ADVISING THE 60+ INVESTOR

The *Wiley Financial Advisor* Series

Advising the 60+ Investor: Tax and Financial Planning Strategies
    by Darlene Smith, Dale Pulliam, and Holland Tolles
Tax-Smart Investing: Maximizing Your Client's Profits
    by Andrew Westhem and Stuart Weissman
Managing Family Trusts: Taking Control of Inherited Wealth
    by Rob Rikoon with Larry Waschka

ADVISING THE 60+ INVESTOR

Tax and Financial Planning Strategies

Darlene Smith, Dale Pulliam, Holland Tolles

John Wiley & Sons, Inc.

New York • Chichester • Weinheim • Brisbane • Singapore • Toronto

Published by John Wiley & Sons, Inc.

Published simultaneously in Canada.

This publication is designed to provide accurate and authoritative information in
regard to the subject matter covered. It is sold with the understanding that neither
the publisher nor the authors are engaged in rendering professional services. If
professional advice or other expert assistance is required, the services of a
competent professional person should be sought.

Library of Congress Cataloging-in-Publication Data:

Smith, Darlene.
    Advising the 60+ investor : tax and financial planning strategies /
Darlene Smith, Dale Pulliam, and Holland Toles.
        p.   cm.—(The Wiley financial advisor series)
    Includes index.
    ISBN 0-471-33353-0 (alk. paper)
    1. Aged—Finance, Personal.   2. Retirement—United States—
Planning.   3. Tax planning—United States.   4. Estate planning—
United States.   I. Pulliam, Dale.   II. Toles, Holland.   III. Title.
IV. Title: Advising the sixty plus investor.   V. Series.
HG179.S5511   1999
332.024'0565—dc21   99-19461

Printed in the United States of America

10 9 8 7 6 5 4 3 2 1

Contents

Introduction

Senior citizens comprise the fastest-growing segment of our population. The baby boomers will soon be reaching retirement age causing the largest short-time increase in senior citizens in our country's history. In addition, most members of this group will live longer than those of any group before them. The result will be a record number of Americans age 60 or older.

A great deal of estate planning has long been practiced with and by this group. However, there are many other financial and tax planning issues that are applicable only to seniors or are particularly important to this group of investor/taxpayers. Approaching retirement presents new challenges both for tax and financial planners and for their clients. Tax professionals often are in a unique position to approach and assist clients nearing retirement, even when the client does not specifically request assistance. Since most individuals visit their tax professional each April, the tax professional has a perfect opportunity to ask a few important questions about the clients' preparation for their new status as retirees. Even a brief conversation while a client signs the tax returns is useful. The purpose of this book is to alert tax and other financial planners to the new tax and financial issues facing clients nearing retirement.

Chapter 1—Financial Planning is a discussion of financial planning for older individuals. Topics included in the discussion are:

- Asset allocation

- Insurance requirements

- Other topics such as reverse mortgages

Chapter 2—Pension and Annuity Income is a discussion of distribution options from retirement plans, the taxability of these distributions, and other topics relating to retirement income. The topics include:

- Taxation of annuities

- Taxation of lump-sum distributions

- Individual retirement accounts, including Roth IRAs

- Required distributions from retirement plans and IRAs

- Additional taxes, such as the tax on early distributions

Chapter 3—Social Security Benefits is a discussion of the benefits available to seniors under our old-age, survivors, and disability benefit system (better know as Social Security) and the income taxation of Social Security benefits. The topics include:

- The amount of the benefits

- Benefits for the worker, the family, and survivors

- Medicare and Medicaid

- Benefits included in gross income

Chapter 4—Transfer of a Closely Held Business is a discussion of issues related to owning closely held businesses and transferring control and/or ownership of the family business to the next generation. The topics include:

- Planning implications of the various entities that may hold the family business—proprietorships, partnerships, and corporations

- Private annuities

- Family limited partnerships

- Estate planning issues for businesses transferred at death

Chapter 5—Estate Planning is a short discussion of the estate and gift transfer tax system and some selected estate planning strategies. Many estate planning implications are discussed in relation to specific topics throughout the book. The topics included in this discussion are:

- A quick overview of the transfer tax system, including the gift tax, the estate tax, and the generation-skipping tax

- The basic goals of estate planning

- The basics of an estate plan

- Basic marital deduction planning

- Grantor-retained interest trusts

Chapter 6—Marriage and Remarriage is a discussion of topics that should be considered prior to a marriage. The topics include:

- The marriage penalty

- Social Security benefits

- Estate planning

- Maximizing the exclusion of gain on the sale of both partners' homes

Chapter 7—Miscellaneous Provisions is a discussion of various other tax issues affecting older taxpayers. The topics include:

- The additional standard deduction

- The credit for the elderly and disabled

- Deductible medical expenses

- Multiple-support agreements

- Exclusions related to disability income, railroad retirement, and military retirement

- Life insurance proceeds

- Endowment contract proceeds

- Tax consequences of volunteerism

- Social Security taxes withheld and paid for household employees

This book is designed to provide financial and tax practitioners with practical insights into the planning opportunities for seniors or near-seniors. The tax laws affecting each of these topics will be discussed in detail, with suggestions and examples provided for enhancing financial and tax planning for senior citizens.

Any tax planning transactions contemplated after consulting this book should be carefully researched. Specific transactions will often include provisions not contemplated by the authors. In addition, as everyone that works with tax law understands, the law is constantly changing. Small changes in the tax law can have large effects on a given transaction. Any action taken based on advice from this book should be evaluated for any tax law changes that may have occurred after this book was published.

ADVISING THE 60+ INVESTOR

Financial Planning

This chapter is designed to provide the tax professional or other financial advisor with an overview of important financial planning and investment issues for people nearing or in retirement. Since clients often turn to their tax professional for advice on these matters, it is important for tax advisors to be aware of the important issues and questions.

Tax professionals have often been serving clients for several years and are therefore in a good position to understand a client's financial picture in an objective manner. It is important to become aware of potential problems before they become problems—rather than doing so after the fact.

The key issues are as follows:

- Does the retiree have enough investment assets to provide the desired retirement income (after considering other sources of retirement income, such as Social Security and company pensions)?

- Will the client, spending at current levels, outlive his or her income?

/   ■ Is the client's investment portfolio structured in a way that is appropriate for his or her financial situation?

This chapter is designed to help the advisor approach these questions.

The first part of this chapter is a discussion of asset allocation and investment considerations relevant for those at or in retirement. If the reader desires detailed information on topics regarding investments and portfolio management, excellent sources are available (see Zvi Bodie, Alex Kane, and Alan J. Marcus, *Investments*, second edition, Homewood/Boston: Irwin, 1993; and John L. Maginn, CFA, and Donald L. Tuttle, CFA, eds., *Managing Investment Portfolios*, second edition, Charlottesville: Association for Investment Management and Research, 1990). Considerations regarding insurance are reviewed. Finally, other sources of income, such as reverse mortgages, are considered. For detailed information on financial planning topics, excellent sources are also available (see David M. Cordell, ed., *Fundamentals of Financial Planning,* third edition, Bryn Mawr, PA: The American College, 1996).

Asset Allocation

The Importance of Asset Allocation

Asset allocation refers to the mixture of broad asset classes in an investor's portfolio. In a simplistic sense, one can think of asset allocation as the overall ratio of bonds versus stocks in the investor's portfolio. An aggressive, growth-oriented portfolio (designed for a younger investor saving for retirement) might contain as much as 80% stocks. Short-run safety of principal would be sacrificed for longer-term growth opportunities. On the other hand, someone in retirement, who needs his or her portfolio to provide significant levels of income on a relatively risk-free basis, would hold a greater percentage of bonds and other income-producing investments in his or her portfolio, perhaps 80% or more in many cases. Stability of capital would be much more important for such an investor.

Asset allocation has a tremendous impact on the risk and return characteristics of a portfolio. Studies have shown that about 90% of a portfolio's risk/return profile is determined by asset allocation, and only about 10% by the actual securities that were selected within the broad asset classes. Therefore, it is important to focus on the client's overall portfolio mix, and not necessarily on his or her individual security holdings.

Setting appropriate asset allocation guidelines requires a review of the client's investment objectives and constraints. A portfolio can then be designed to best meet these needs. These objectives and constraints are discussed in the next section.

Investor Objectives and Constraints

Return Requirements and Risk Tolerance

What are the client's objectives with regard to rate of return and risk tolerance? Obviously, all investors want high returns without taking risk, but the laws of economics usually prevail against such outcomes. Sadly, to achieve higher returns, investors must be prepared and willing to bear higher levels of risk. Perhaps the best place to start when examining an appropriate asset allocation is the investor's risk tolerance. Is the client bothered by fluctuations in value of his or her portfolio? Has the client tended to focus on safe or insured investments in the past, or does he or she have experience with riskier investments? Some clients may have discovered equities fairly recently, and as a result may have unrealistic expectations regarding the risk of these investments. On the other hand, those who experienced the 1970s and the associated debacle in financial assets are aware of the downside risk of bonds and stocks.

What are the investor's return requirements? Consideration must be given to the client's level of wealth, other sources of retirement income, and goals regarding retirement lifestyle.

X   Retirees need to earn a return high enough to produce the necessary income over time, but their assets also need to grow to offset
inflation. However, a client's desired rate of return, given realistic
capital market expectations, may not be achievable in some cases
without taking inappropriate levels of risk. In such cases, retirees
may need to reduce spending requirements in conjunction with
accepting a lower but safer return on investment.

    In addition, given the success investors have had with finan-
cial assets over the better of two decades, it is not uncommon for
clients (and investment professionals) to have unrealistic expectations about the risk/return nature of the financial markets
going forward. More will be devoted to this issue later.

Constraints

The retiree's investment portfolio needs to satisfy risk/return
requirements within the context of various constraints.

    How much income does the client's portfolio need to pro-
duce? Investors who need significant levels of income need to be
positioned in more of a "distribution" mode, rather than an
"accumulation" mode. Income-producing securities and higher-
dividend-yielding stocks (and mutual funds that pursue those
investments) would be more appropriate than growth-oriented
investments. This is because, if the investor were heavily positioned in equities, income requirements would necessitate a certain amount of liquidation of stocks if the dividend yield does not
generate enough income. Forced liquidation of equities in a bear
market, however, will do great damage to the intended long-run
rate of return. Although some exposure to equities is warranted for
most investors, clients who require significant cash distributions
should position their portfolios to exhibit less volatility.

    What is the investor's time horizon? Retirees may seem to
have short time horizons, but in reality they need to plan as if
they will live to ripe old ages. They do not want to outlive their
income. Investors who have longer time horizons can generally
afford to be more aggressive and should seek growth. Younger
investors saving for retirement are often encouraged to maintain

extremely growth-oriented portfolios. This is because they have time to ride out the ups and downs in the stock market, and also because they can correct for investment mistakes by saving more and working more. On the other hand, those already in retirement should adopt a more conservative approach to their portfolios. If they must rely heavily on their investments to provide retirement income, they cannot afford significant short-run losses in their portfolios caused by overexposure to equities. Reductions in the value of the portfolio will necessitate reductions in spending levels.

Investors with very short time horizons require much more safety of principal. It should be noted that those in their 60s, although at retirement age, should not necessarily be viewed as having short time horizons. They may need their portfolio to provide income over a period of 40 years or more.

Tax considerations play an important role in determining appropriate investments for retirees. Those whose investments are concentrated in tax-deferred retirement plans have the luxury of avoiding taxes on their investments until income is distributed. If investors have investments outside of tax-advantaged plans, taxes must be considered.

One important area where the investor's tax situation must be considered is the decision whether to invest in municipal bonds or taxable bonds. To examine whether a client should invest in municipal securities instead of taxable counterparts, one can calculate the *taxable equivalent yield* on a municipal bond as follows:

$$\text{Taxable equivalent yield} = \frac{\text{yield on municipal bond}}{(1 - \text{marginal tax rate})}$$

The taxable equivalent yield can be compared to the yield on an equivalent-risk corporate bond to see which one will produce the highest yield on an after-tax basis. Since municipal bonds have default risk, care should be taken when comparing their yields with U.S. Treasury bond yields.

A similar measure, the *tax rate of indifference,* is calculated as follows:

$$\text{Tax rate of indifference} = 1 - \frac{\text{yield on municipal bond}}{\text{yield on equivalent risk corporate bond}}$$

The tax rate of indifference is the marginal tax rate that would make an investor indifferent between municipal bonds and equivalent-risk corporate bonds. If an investor's marginal tax rate is above the tax rate of indifference, the investor would generally be better off investing in municipal bonds when taxes are taken into consideration. The tax rate of indifference should be calculated for various maturity ranges. Generally, the indifference tax rate is higher in the shorter maturity ranges, due to the domination of corporate investors in that segment of the municipal market. However, in the long-term end of the market the tax rate has hovered at about 25% or below, making municipals advantageous for many investors.

It should be noted, however, that municipal bond investors bear tax risk (the risk in this case is that tax rates would be reduced, or that the tax-exempt status of municipal bonds would be eliminated). While tax risk seems remote at the moment, the municipal market has been rocked in the past by such factors, particularly in the time prior to the Tax Reform Act of 1986. Investors should be aware of this source of risk.

Other considerations should also be considered. Do clients desire to bequeath an estate to their heirs, or are they willing to spend down to low levels of wealth if they live long enough? Are there special goals with regard to charitable contributions, travel, helping with their grandchildren's education, and so forth? In such cases, cash distributions must be less than the rate of return earned on the portfolio in order to provide growth of income and preservation or even growth of current wealth.

Realistic Capital Market Expectations

Investors must take care not to incorporate unrealistic expectations about future capital market performance into their return and risk outlook. Many investors expect to continue to receive returns of 15% to 20% annually going forward. This is unrealistic, given valuations levels in the U.S. stock market in 1998. Investors often tend to extrapolate the immediate past into the future and, led by investment professionals who fall victim to the same human nature, may aggressively invest in equities (a policy that has enjoyed great success in the recent past).

However, an examination of the current investment fundamentals brings a more sobering view to the case for equities. With dividend yields at an all-time low and price/earnings (P/E) ratios high (about 1.5% and 25x, respectively, on the Standard and Poor's 500 Index), extremely high returns will be very difficult to obtain. One can estimate the expected long-run annualized return on common stocks as follows:

$$\text{Expected return} = \frac{\text{expected dividend}}{\text{market price}} + \text{expected long-run dividend growth}$$

The dividend divided by the market price is the expected dividend yield, and the long-run expected dividend (and earnings) growth is the expected capital gains yield. Investors in common stocks receive their returns from two sources: the dividend yield, and the price appreciation, which depends on earnings growth.

For the S&P 500, the dividend yield is about 1.5%, and if you estimate long-run earnings growth at 9% (which many would argue is unrealistic in a mature economy with slower growth and low inflation), the expected rate of return is:

$$\text{Expected return} = 1.5\% + 9\% = 10.5\%$$

This is a far cry from the returns enjoyed in recent years, but it is still good compared to what is available in the bond market. (The 30-year Treasury bond currently yields about 5%.) In the current low inflation environment, 10.5% is a good rate of return after inflation, especially when one thinks in terms of real returns.

The danger is, however, that fluctuations in valuation levels in the financial markets could produce poor returns over short-

and even longer-term periods (10 years or more). The return estimated in the previous paragraph depends on achieving earnings and dividend growth of 9% (which again many would argue is unrealistic). Just as important, the 10.5% return requires valuation levels to remain as high as they are now (1.5% yield and 25x earnings) when the investor needs to liquidate. Even if earnings and dividends actually grew at 9% per year, but the P/E fell to 15x, the realized capital gains return over a 10-year period would be only 3.57%. The 10.5% return in this context becomes a return that would only occur if everything goes perfectly.

The problem with poor returns over the short run depends on the investor's time horizon, and the extent to which he or she relies on equities as an investment vehicle. Younger investors who are using equities to save for retirement can view a weak market as an opportunity to purchase stocks at inexpensive prices. However, a weak market could hurt someone in retirement who has to liquidate some equities each year to provide part of their income. In addition, returns over shorter periods (such as 10 years) become much more important to investors in retirement.

Investors need to realize that the reason stock returns have been so high over the past few decades is that we have been in bull market with rising valuations. Interest rates started out above 15% and are now below 5%. P/E ratios started the bull market at about 10x and are now 25x. The rise in the P/E is due to the decline in inflation and interest rates. While we can hopefully count on the U.S. economy and American companies to continue to expand in the long run, we cannot count on ever-rising P/E ratios.

Investors, especially less wealthy ones, should carefully consider their exposure to equities. While equities are desirable for their ability to outperform inflation in the long run, the danger for retirees is overexposure, which can cause tremendous problems down the road. Care must be taken to ensure an adequate long-run income level.

Selecting Appropriate Asset Classes

This section focuses on the important characteristics of the major asset classes. In order to determine the appropriate weights to attach to each asset class in the investor's overall portfolio, it is important to understand how each asset class works.

Equities

Equities are needed in a portfolio in order to produce long-term returns above inflation. Equities comprise the only financial asset class that has demonstrated significantly higher returns over inflation in the long run. Almost everyone who needs their portfolio to produce income would find some equities necessary to provide the growth needed to outpace inflation. However, due to their volatility, equities are more appropriate during the accumulation phase than during the distribution phase of the investor's life cycle.

Hopefully, clients had adequate equity exposure during their accumulation years. But, while an 80% allocation to equities may be appropriate for a young investor, 60% equities might be on the high end for someone at retirement age, and depending on the investor's wealth level, this percentage may need to be reduced even further. In general, as the client gets older, less and less of the portfolio (if it's needed as a source of income) should be allocated to equities.

Bonds

Bonds would be placed in a portfolio to produce income and to lessen the overall volatility of the portfolio. When investing in bonds, the issue becomes whether to choose short-term or long-term investments. The key to making this determination is the balance between *price risk* and *reinvestment rate risk.* Price risk refers to the fact that bond values change when interest rates change, and are inversely related to interest rates. If interest rates rise, bond prices fall—and vice versa. The risk that rates would rise, causing bond prices to fall, is referred to as price risk. Price risk is greater for longer-term, smaller coupon bonds. For example, a 6% coupon, 30-year bond will decline in value by a little more than 10% if interest rates rise by 1%. While investors who are using bonds to provide a long-term income stream may not worry about these fluctuations, investors with short time horizons are subject to great price risk if they invest their money in long-term bonds.

On the other hand, investors who need income over longer periods of time are taking substantial reinvestment rate risk if they invest in bonds with relatively short maturities. The extreme example would be the investor who is using one-year Treasury bills or CDs to generate income over long periods of time. Since the investor must reinvest the funds each year, the risk is that rates would fall substantially when it is time to reinvest, thereby causing the investor's income level to drop. Investors who stayed with shorter-term bonds in the 1980s saw their interest return fall from the teens to low single digits by the early 1990s. More recently, investors who balked at locking in rates as low as 7% now find that the rates on even long-term bonds are now about 5%.

The bottom line is that investors who need their portfolios to produce income over longer periods should be more inclined to invest in long-term bonds to avoid reinvestment rate risk. Some amount of short-term bonds and even money market securities (maturities less than one year) should be kept to provide liquidity. Otherwise, it is probably wise to accept the price risk of longer-term bonds in order to provide a more stable income stream.

The big danger of bond investing, especially during the current lower interest rates, is that of an unexpected increase in inflation. The long-term Treasury bond, now yielding about 5%, is pricing expectations of very low inflation. If the bond market is wrong about inflation, then bond investors will get hurt, much as they did in the 1970s. In order to hedge this risk, investors should look for some assets for their portfolios that will provide protection against inflation. These might include real estate investment trusts, inflation-indexed bonds, and other potential inflation hedges.

Think After-Tax, After-Inflation

Many investors focus on nominal, pretax returns and not on real, after-tax returns. Investors must account for the tax penalty as well as the penalty for loss of purchasing power, or inflation. There are some common misconceptions when dealing with this issue.

The real return (the return the investor earns after inflation) is often defined as follows:

$$\text{Real return} = \text{nominal return} - \text{inflation}$$

Assuming a 5% nominal return and 2% inflation, the real return would be 5% minus 2%, or 3%. However, many would quickly point out that this calculation ignores taxes. If the investor is in the 28% tax bracket, the real after-tax return would be as follows:

$$\text{Real after-tax return} = \text{nominal return} (1 - T) - \text{inflation}$$

$$= 5\%(.72) - 2\%$$

$$= 3.6\% - 2\%$$

$$= 1.6\%$$

Uncle Sam taxes the nominal return, and the investor is not allowed a deduction for inflation, so the after-tax real return is only 1.6%. This underscores the need to outperform inflation over the long run. Equities provide an advantage over inflation that cannot be ignored, given the favorable tax treatment afforded to capital gains returns (capital gains are not taxed until realized). The tax-deferred growth provides equities with additional advantage over inflation relative to fixed-income securities.

Mutual Funds—Factors to Consider

In order to get adequate diversification, most investors turn to mutual funds. Mutual funds provide significant advantages in this regard by enabling investors to obtain diversified stock and bond portfolios with small amounts of investment dollars. However, in considering appropriate funds for the portfolio, several important issues should be considered.

Sales Charges

Often, mutual funds sold by commission brokers involve up-front sales charges or *loads*. Load funds may charge the investor 3% to 5% or more up front in order to compensate brokers for selling the fund to investors. In addition, many funds levy an annual marketing fee (a 12b-1 charge) of 0.25%, which is used to continue to compensate the fund salesperson. These fees cut into the investor's return, and can be avoided in many no-load fund families.

Expense Ratio

The *expense ratio* refers to the percentage cost charged to the investor, to compensate the fund manager and management company. Expense ratios can range as low as 0.25% for index funds (funds that simply attempt to replicate the return on a broad index of securities), and as high as 2% or more for actively managed funds. The expense ratio also reduces the investor's return. Funds are required to report returns earned by the investor after expenses, so these charges are reflected in fund performance numbers. In an efficient market, however, one would expect lower expense-ratio funds to produce higher rates of return for the investor over the long run.

Trading Costs

While mutual funds are large institutional investors and generally pay much lower commissions than individual investors, one must be aware of two hidden costs of trading—the *bid/ask spread* and *price concessions*. Investors who trade over-the-counter stocks pay not only a commission to a broker, but also are subject to the dealer's bid/ask spread. For less actively traded securities, the dealer spread can be a significant percentage of the investment. In addition, large institutions are subject to price concessions as they attempt to acquire and liquidate large positions. Institutional investors who are trading large quantities of securities will tend to move the price as a result of their trading. When you look at the total cost of trading (the sum of commissions, bid/ask spreads, and price concessions), it is clear that excessive portfolio turnover can cut into the investor's rate of return. Mutual funds with high turnover have the hurdle of higher trading costs to overcome.

Tax Efficiency

Another area where trading produces a drag on portfolio returns is in taxation of investment returns. Funds that have high turnover ratios generally realize more capital gains—which are required to be reported by the fund holders and result in tax liability. Excessive realized capital gains reduce the tax-deferral advantage of equities. Since mutual fund returns are reported on a pretax basis, investors must be aware of the effect of excessive trading. Funds with high turnover ratios generally cause greater tax incidence for their investors.

Investors must also be wary of purchasing funds whose portfolios contain large unrealized capital gains. Regardless of whether the investor participated in these gains, he or she is responsible for the tax liability when the gains are reported. This could be a real problem if mutual fund redemptions cause mutual funds to liquidate security positions. Even tax-efficient funds (such as index funds), which minimize trading, are subject to this potential problem. This issue therefore is of extreme importance to taxable investors. On the bright side, investors whose mutual fund investments are in tax-deferred retirement accounts are immune from the problem of excessive realized gains.

Choosing an Investment Professional

Depending on the sophistication of the client, an investment professional may be needed to assist the client in developing a successful investment program. The key choices are between commission-based brokers and fee-based investment advisors.

With full-service commission brokers, one must watch for conflict of interest. Brokers, no matter what they may say, are paid to trade. Given their need to generate transactions in order to make a living, they may encourage the client to engage in excessive, tax-inefficient trading in the investment portfolio. Full-service brokers can be useful to clients who are sophisticated enough to make their own investment decisions and just need a little extra advice and help. Caution must be taken, however, before relying solely on a commission broker as a financial advisor. Generally, brokers have too many clients and are too focused on generating transactions to really take every client's specific needs into account. Also, brokers are not always adequately trained to have complete control of an investor's finances.

On the other end of the spectrum, fee-based investment advisors generally are given power of attorney to make and execute investment decisions in the client's account. Compensated on a percentage of assets under management, rather than on commissions, fee-based advisors are generally held to have less conflict of interest. Since they are not compensated by commissions, they have no incentive to engage in excessive trading or to market specific products. Usually trading in the client's account through a broker at discounted institutional commission rates, the investment advisor "sits on the same side of the table" as the client. Fee-based advisors are appropriate for investors who need more help with their investments or who do not want to take the time to worry about their investments on an ongoing basis. Care must be taken to ensure that the advisor is honest, highly trained, and experienced in various market environments. The advisor's fees should be reasonable as well. In today's marketplace, fees in excess of 1% are probably too high, especially when one realistically considers the rates of return that will be available in coming years. Many advisors routinely charge 1.5% to 2%. Fees are always negotiable, so clients should shop around, comparing both quality and price.

Conclusion

Financial planning for those in retirement involves setting realistic spending goals in the context of a realistic capital market outlook, and an appropriate allocation of investment resources. Asset allocation determines 90% of a portfolio's risk and return characteristics and is much more important than the security selection decision. The investor's asset allocation should be designed within the parameters of return requirements and constraints such as wealth, time horizon, liquidity needs, and tax considerations.

The retiree's investment portfolio needs to ensure an appropriate level of income and allow for growth of income to offset inflation. However, for investors with less wealth and shorter time horizons, the risk of the portfolio should be carefully considered. If the portfolio is to provide a stable source of income, the lower returns of safer investments must be accepted.

Insurance Considerations

What types of insurance should retirees consider purchasing? Insurance needs differ dramatically during a person's lifetime. Young people with no dependents have little need for life insurance. Young families living on one or two incomes obviously have considerable need for life insurance. Health insurance, while expensive, can avoid catastrophic loss in the event of major illness. The key is to weigh the costs and benefits of various insurance products to determine whether they are needed.

Life Insurance

Life insurance is not as necessary for those in retirement. Life insurance proceeds are designed to provide investment assets for income protection in the event of the untimely death of an income earner and to provide liquidity for estate tax planning purposes. After reviewing their life insurance needs, retirees may be able to cancel policies to reduce unnecessary expenses.

In addition, all or part of the cash value of a whole or universal life policy can be accessed to provide additional income.

Annuities

Annuities can be purchased that will provide lifetime income for an individual or for the individual and spouse. Annuities may be useful for those with limited investment resources, in order to reduce the risk of their outliving their investment income.

Health Insurance

Health care costs rise significantly as a person gets older, and the probability of lengthy and expensive illness increases. Medicare reimbursements generally leave seniors with significant out-of-pocket expenses. This risk can be managed by purchasing insurance that is designed to supplement Medicare coverage and to provide coverage for medical costs not covered by Medicare.

Long-Term Care

Medicare provides limited coverage for long-term care needs, such as a nursing home. Several insurance products have been developed that will provide long-term care coverage. Also, home health care services are proliferating, providing alternatives to traditional long-term care needs.

Other Issues in Financial Planning

Hopefully, when expenses are realistically considered and all sources of retirement income are combined, retirees will be able to achieve their desired lifestyle with peace of mind. Income needs are significant, and the risk of inflation affecting living expenses must be considered. Seniors who face tight budgets should carefully consider how to reduce expenses and maximize retirement income. This section provides some additional ideas that may be useful in reaching this goal.

Working Longer: Postretirement Employment

Retiring at age 65 is a relatively new concept. Until recent years, the life expectancy of the average American was not much past 65 years. Now, due to various factors, Americans generally are living longer and healthier lives. The golden years now may provide several years during which a retiree can live an active and productive life. In many professions, there is no real reason why people cannot continue to work well into their 70s, 80s, or even longer, providing additional years of income during which savings can continue to be built up for eventual retirement.

Retirees who have left their careers may be able to find part-time jobs, which may be rewarding and provide significant income while still allowing for plenty of free time to pursue leisure activities. Professionals who have left their jobs on a full-time basis may be able to find consulting work or special projects where their expertise is needed and will be well rewarded. Clients should be urged to pursue such opportunities. Such activities will not only provide additional income but will enhance the self-esteem and probably extend the life of the retiree.

Accessing Real Estate Equity

A person's equity investment in his or her dwelling may be one of the largest assets in their overall portfolio. This asset may need to be used to provide additional retirement income. This source of income may be particularly important for someone whose retirement budget is tight. One option is to trade down to a smaller, less expensive house in order to free up additional investment capital for retirement. A retired couple may be living in a large house that was designed for a large family. By trading down, they not only will be able to enjoy a larger retirement income but will also save money on utilities and taxes. In addition, if retirees are living in an area where the cost of living is high, they may be able to significantly improve their standard of living by relocating to a less expensive area of the country. Anecdotes of California retirees who sell their modest homes for very high prices and move to other areas of the country are common.

For some, however, the thought of leaving a home filled with many years of memories and where friends are nearby is unbearable. A reverse-annuity mortgage may be an option in these cases. In a reverse-annuity mortgage, the homeowner sells an interest in the equity of his or her home in exchange for a stream of payments. In this way, the retiree is able to access the equity in the home to increase income without having to sell the property and relocate. The reverse mortgage can be structured to provide a lifetime annuity that remains in effect until the death of one or both spouses.

CHAPTER 2

Pension and Annuity Income

After carefully saving for many years, seniors are ready to begin reaping the benefits of their retirement plans and using the benefits to provide for their daily living expenses and, hopefully, for such long-awaited retirement goals as travel and other recreation. Distributions from these plans are generally totally or partially taxable. At some point, distributions are mandatory to avoid penalties. The following paragraphs discuss the taxability of the distributions and the various penalties to be avoided.

Taxation of Periodic Payments—Annuities

Introduction

An *annuity* is a series of payments under a contract. An individual may be entitled to an annuity for a variety of reasons:

- The individual may purchase an annuity contract.

- A participant in some qualified employee pension or profit-sharing plans may elect to receive all or part of the benefits as an annuity.

- A beneficiary of a life insurance contract may elect to receive the benefit as an annuity.

Types of Annuities

Types of annuities include:

- *Fixed-period annuities,* where the individual receives fixed amounts at regular intervals for a fixed period of time
- *Single-life annuities,* where the individual receives fixed amounts at regular intervals for life, with the payments ending at his or her death
- *Joint and survivor annuities,* where the individual and then the individual's joint annuitant (after the individual's death) receive fixed amounts at regular intervals for the life of the individual and then for the life of the surviving joint annuitant
- *Variable annuities,* where the individual receives amounts that may vary in amount (based upon attributes such as profitability or cost-of-living adjustments) for a fixed amount of time or for life

Taxation of Annuities

Exclusion Ratio

In some cases, all of the annuity is subject to taxation when received. In other cases, a portion of each annuity payment is treated as a return of the recipient's investment and is not taxable. The nontaxable portion is determined by the following exclusion ratio:

$$\text{Excluded portion of annuity} = \frac{\text{investment in contract}}{\text{expected return}}$$

Investment in the Contract

An individual's investment in the contract is the amount of premiums or other consideration paid for the contract with after-tax dollars. Employees have no investment in qualified pension or profit plans where the employer payments into the plan were not taxable or where the employee made payments into the plan with pretax dollars. Amounts paid into Sec. 401(k) plans are pretax dollars and do not result in investment in the contract. Amounts contributed by the employer that were included in the individual's gross income are included in the individual's investment.

If the annuity has a refund feature, the investment in the contract must be reduced by the present value of the refund feature. (See Sec. 72(c)(2).) A refund feature exists if (1) the expected return under the contract depends in whole or in part on the life expectancy of one or more individuals, (2) the contract provides for payments to be made to a beneficiary (or the estate of an annuitant) on or after the death of the annuitant if a specified amount or a stated number of payments have not been paid to the annuitant or annuitants prior to death, and (3) such payments are in the nature of a refund of the consideration paid. The computation of the present value of this feature is found in Treasury Regulation Section 1.72-7.

Expected Return

The expected return of a fixed-period annuity is the amount of the periodic payment multiplied by the number of periods the benefit will be paid.

The expected return for an annuity based on the life of one or more individuals is determined by multiplying the periodic payment by a factor determined by using Reg. Sec. 1.72-9. The regulation contains tables to determine the life expectancy for an individual or the joint life expectancy for two individuals.

In 1986, the gender-specific tables to determine life expectancy were replaced with unisex tables. If investment in the contract was made both before and after June 30, 1986, an election can be made to use both the pre-July 1986 and the post-June 1986 tables. (See Reg. Sec. 1.72 (d)(6).) The exclusion ratio is the sum of two exclusion ratios computed separately. The exclusion ratio with respect to the pre-July 1986 investment in the contract is determined by dividing the pre-July investment in the contract by the expected return determined by using the pre-July 1986 tables in Reg. Sec. 1.72-9. The exclusion ratio with respect to the post-June 1986 investment in the contract is determined by dividing the post-June investment in the contract by the expected return determined by using the post-June 1986 tables in Reg. Sec. 1.72-9. (See Sec. 72.)

COMPUTATION AID: For a worksheet to compute the excluded portion of an annuity, see Worksheet 2.1 on page 52.

EXAMPLES

Mr. Smith purchased an annuity contract providing for monthly payments of $100 for 15 years. He paid $12,650 for the contract. The expected return is $18,000 ($100 × 15 years × 12 months per year). The exclusion ratio is 70.278% ($12,650/$18,000). If 12 monthly payments are received in a year by Mr. Smith, he may exclude $843.34 ($1,200 × .70278). The balance of $356.66 ($1,200.00 − 843.34) is the amount to be included in gross income.

Ms. Jones, an unmarried individual, purchased an annuity contract after 1986 for $19,000. Beginning in the year Ms. Jones becomes 65, the contract will provide $100 per month for Ms. Jones's life. Using Table V in Reg. Sec. 1.72-9, Ms. Jones has an expected return multiple of 20.0. The expected return is $24,000 ($100 × 20 years × 12 months per year). The exclusion ratio is 79.167% ($19,000/$24,000). If 12 monthly payments are received in a year by Ms. Jones, she may exclude $949.64 ($1,200 × .79167). The balance of $250.36 ($1,200.00 − 949.64) is the amount to be included in gross income.

Mr. and Ms. Jones purchased an annuity contract after 1986 for $21,000. Beginning in the year the couple both become 65, the contract will provide $100 per month to the couple while both are living, and then $100 per month for the life of the surviving spouse. Using Table VI in Reg. Sec. 1.72-9, Mr. and Ms. Jones have an expected return multiple of 25.0. The expected return is $30,000 ($100 × 25 years × 12 months per year). The exclusion ratio is 70% ($21,000/$30,000). If 12 monthly payments are received in a year by Ms. Jones, she may exclude $840.00 ($1,200 × .70). The balance of $360.00 ($1,200.00 − 840.00) is the amount to be included in gross income.

Excluded Amounts Must Equal Investment

When the individual has excluded amounts equal to the investment in the contract, additional payments are totally taxable. If the individual dies before excluding amounts equal to the investment in the contract, the remaining unrecovered investment is deducted on the individual's final tax return as a miscellaneous itemized deduction not subject to the 2% of adjusted gross income reduction. This deduction is treated as a trade or business deduction in determining a net operating loss deduction. (See Sec. 72(b).)

Simplified Method

A simplified method for determining the excludable portion of an annuity payment must be used if all of the following conditions apply:

- The starting date of the annuity is after November 18, 1996.

- The payments are being made from a Sec. 401(a) qualified employee plan, a Sec. 403(a) employee annuity, or a Sec. 403(b) tax-sheltered annuity contract.

- The payments are based on the life (or joint life) of the annuitant(s).

- The annuitant is under age 75.

(The general method previously discussed must be used for non-qualified plans. It can be used if the annuity starting date is after July 1, 1986 but before November 19, 1996.)

This simplified method must be used to determine the portion of the annuity payment that represents nontaxable return of basis. By using the correct table, the individual's or combined individuals' expected number of payments is determined. The investment is divided by this number, with the result being the excluded portion of each payment. This method is simple, and may result in a larger excludable amount than the method required under the Sec. 72 regulations. This simplified method does not apply if the primary annuitant is 75 or older on the annuity starting date, unless there are fewer than five years of guaranteed payments under the annuity. (See Sec. 72(d)(1)(E).) No refund feature adjustment is required in computing the individual's investment in the contract for this purpose. (See Sec. 72(d)(1)(C).) Different provisions apply, based on the annuity starting date, for determining the expected number of payments.

For annuity starting dates after December 31, 1997, Sec. 72(d) provides two tables (below) for determining the anticipated payments.

TABLE 2.1 Annuity Payable Over Life of One Person

If the annuity is payable over the life of a single individual, the anticipated payments are determined as follows:

If the age of the annuitant on the annuity starting date is:	The number of anticipated payments is:
Not more than 55	360
More than 55 but not more than 60	310
More than 60 but not more than 65	260
More than 65 but not more than 70	210
More than 70	160

TABLE 2.1a Annuity Payable Over Lives of More Than One Person

If the annuity is payable over the lives of more than one individual, the anticipated payments are determined as follows:

If the combined ages of annuitants are:	The number of anticipated payments is:
Not more than 110	410
More than 110 but not more than 120	360
More than 120 but not more than 130	310
More than 130 but not more than 140	260
More than 140	210

COMPUTATION AID: For a worksheet to compute the excluded portion of an annuity using the simplified method, see Worksheet 2.2 on page 53.

For annuity starting dates after November 18, 1996, and before January 1, 1998, Sec. 72(d) provided only one table for determining the anticipated payments, regardless of the existence of joint annuitants. The anticipated payments were determined as follows:

TABLE 2.2 Annuity Payments—Start Date after Nov 18, 1996/Before Jan 1, 1998

If the age of the primary annuitant on the annuity starting date is:	The number of anticipated payments is:
Not more than 55	360
More than 55 but not more than 60	310
More than 60 but not more than 65	260
More than 65 but not more than 70	210
More than 70	160

For annuity starting dates after July 1, 1986, and before November 19, 1996, another table was provided in IRS Notice 88-118, 1988-2 CB 450. The anticipated payments were determined as follows:

TABLE 2.3 Annuity Payments—Start Date after July 1, 1986/Before Nov 19, 1996

If the age of the primary annuitant on the annuity starting date is:	The number of anticipated payments is:
Not more than 55	300
More than 55 but not more than 60	260
More than 60 but not more than 65	240
More than 65 but not more than 70	170
More than 70	120

EXAMPLE

Upon retirement in 1998, Mr. Wilson begins receiving retirement benefits in the form of a joint and 50% survivor annuity to be paid for the joint lives of Mr. Wilson and Mrs. Wilson, both age 65. The annuity starting date is January 1, 1998. Mr. Wilson purchased the annuity for $31,000 and has received no distributions prior to the annuity starting date. Mr. Wilson will receive a monthly retirement benefit of $1,000 per month for life, and if Mrs. Wilson survives Mr. Wilson, she will receive a monthly survivor benefit of $500 per month for her life after Mr. Wilson's death.

Under the simplified method, Mr. Wilson's investment in the contract is $31,000 (the after-tax contributions to the plan). The set number of monthly payments for distributees whose ages total 130 is 310. The tax-free portion of each $1,000 monthly annuity payment to Mr. Wilson is $100, determined by dividing Mr. Wilson's investment ($31,000) by the number of monthly payments (310). Upon Mr. Wilson's death, if Mr. Wilson has not recovered the full $31,000 investment, Mrs. Wilson will also exclude $100 from each $500 monthly annuity payment. Any annuity payments received after 310 payments have been made will be fully includible in gross income. If Mr. and Mrs. Wilson die before 310 payments have been made, a deduction is allowed for the last income tax return in the amount of the unrecovered investment.

Taxation of Lump-Sum Distributions

Introduction

Distributions from a qualified plan are generally taxable to the employee or the beneficiary when distributed. (See Sec. 402(a).) When received in installments, the distributions are taxable under the annuity rules previously discussed. (See Sec. 402(b).) When the distributions are received as a lump sum, the individual has several options. These options include:

- A rollover of the benefits
- Capital gain treatment
- Five-year or ten-year averaging

Definition of a Lump-Sum Distribution

A lump sum is defined as the distribution or payment within one of the recipient's taxable years of the balance to the credit of an employee which becomes payable to the recipient under one of the following circumstances:

- After a plan participant attains age 59.5 years
- On account of a plan participant's death
- On account of a self-employed participant's disability
- On account of an employee participant's separation from the service of the employer

However, any distribution made during the first five tax years that the employee was a participant in a plan, unless the employee has died, will not qualify as a lump-sum distribution. Distributions from IRA's do not qualify as lump-sum distributions. (See Sec. 402.)

Similar plans must be combined when determining if all of an employee's interest in a plan has been distributed within one taxable year of the recipient. This requires that pension plans, profit-sharing plans, and stock bonus plans be aggregated. Additional aggregation rules apply if multiple lump-sum distributions are received in different years. (See Sec. 402.)

Recovery of Cost Tax Free

A participant may recover his or her cost in the distribution tax free. The cost includes:

- The plan participant's total nondeductible contributions to the plan
- Employer contributions that were taxable to the plan participant
- Repayments of loans that were taxable to the plan participant
- Net unrealized appreciation in employer securities distributed
- The plan participant's taxable costs of any life insurance contract distributed

Subject to qualifications, the recipient of a lump-sum distribution has several options as to the tax treatment of the distribution. These options include:

- Roll over all or part of the distribution

- Report the entire taxable part of the distribution as ordinary income

- Report the part of the distribution from participation before 1974 as a capital gain and the amount from participation after 1973 as ordinary income

- Use 5-year or 10-year averaging on the total taxable amount

- Use 5-year or 10-year averaging on the part of the distribution from participation after 1973 and report the part of the distribution from participation before 1974 as a capital gain. (See Sec. 402.)

Rollover

A rollover is a withdrawal of cash or other assets from one qualified retirement plan or IRA and its reinvestment in another qualified retirement plan or IRA. The reinvestment must be made within 60 days after the distribution is received. Any part of the distribution that is not reinvested must be included in gross income. Income averaging or capital gain treatment is not available for portions of the distribution not reinvested. (See Sec. 402.) If noncash assets are received, the same property must be rolled over. (See Sec. 408.)

Rollovers from one IRA to another IRA and from one qualified plan to another qualified plan are allowed. A conduit IRA may be used to move assets from one qualified plan to another qualified plan. The conduit IRA can hold only the assets rolled into it, plus assets attributable to the reinvestment of earnings of those assets. Distributions that have been placed in an IRA no longer qualify for averaging. (See Sec. 408.)

A participant may roll over distributions from each IRA to another IRA only once a year. (See Prop. Reg. Sec. 1.408-4(b)(4).)

Capital Gain Treatment

In some cases, the amount of the distribution attributable to participation before 1974 can be treated as a capital gain. The remaining distribution attributable to participation after 1973 is treated as ordinary income. If the individual qualifies for 5- or 10-year averaging, this portion of the distribution may be averaged. (See Sec. 402.)

Capital gain treatment is available only if the individual was born before 1936. The gain is taxable at the rate of 20%. Capital gain treatment can only be elected once by any plan participant.

A similar allocation must be made for federal estate tax attributable to the distribution.

The individual may elect to treat the capital gain portion of the distribution as ordinary so that this portion of the distribution is subject to the averaging option. However, the election is irrevocable and will apply to any later lump-sum distributions. (See Sec. 402.)

Five- or Ten-Year Averaging

Ten-year averaging is available only if the individual was born before 1936. Five-year averaging is available only if the individual was born before 1936 or has attained age 59½ years of age. The tax under the 5-year option is computed using the current year's tax rates. The tax under the 10-year option is computed using 1986 rates. Both use rates for a single individual. The employee must have been a participant in the plan for five or more years to be eligible for averaging, unless the distribution is due to the employee's death. Each optional method can only be elected once by any plan participant. The amount subject to averaging for both methods is the portion of the distribution subject to averaging over a minimum distribution allowance. The minimum distribution allowance is (1) the lesser of $10,000 or one-half the amount subject to averaging, reduced by (2) 20% of the amount by which the amount subject to averaging exceeds $20,000. The minimum distribution allowance is reduced to zero for distributions in excess of $70,000. (See Sec. 402.)

The Tax Relief Act of 1997 repealed the 5-year averaging option. It will not be available for distributions made after December 31, 1999.

COMPUTATION AID: For a worksheet to compute taxes on a lump-sum distribution, see Worksheet 2.3 on page 54.

EXAMPLE

Mr. Smith, born in 1930, retired from Excel Corporation in 1998. Mr. Smith elected to withdraw the entire amount to his credit from the company's retirement plan. In December, 1998, he received a distribution of $175,000. This amount represented $25,000 attributable to his own nondeductible contributions and $150,000 attributable to Excel's contributions. The portion of the distribution attributable to Mr. Smith's participation prior to 1974 was $10,000.

The ordinary income portion of the distribution was $140,000. Mr. Smith can elect either 5-year or 10-year averaging. These taxes are computed as follows:

5-year averaging

$140,000 × 20% = $28,000

Tax = $3,802.50 + (28% of [$28,000 − $25,350]) = $4,544.50

Multiply by 5 = $22,722.50

10-year averaging

$140,000 × 10% = $14,000

Tax = $2,160.30 + (23% of [$14,000 − $13,710]) = $2,227

Multiply by 10 = $22,270

Lesser of 5-year averaging and 10-year averaging =	$22,270
Add: Capital gain tax − $10,000 × 20% =	2,000
Total tax on lump-sum distribution =	$24,270

Rollover or Lump-Sum Treatment?

In some cases, individuals should seriously consider rolling over their lump-sum distribution rather than using the special averaging methods. If the averaging method results in substantial taxes, the tax-free earnings within an IRA can result in substantially greater distributions over a period of years. For smaller distributions with a smaller tax bite, averaging may be more appropriate. Each case should be carefully evaluated based upon the individual's needs.

COMPUTATION AID: For a worksheet to compare the effect of a rollover to a lump-sum distribution, see Worksheet 2.4 on page 56.

EXAMPLE

Ms. Anderson, age 65, receives a lump-sum distribution of $750,000. She wants to begin receiving annual distributions, after tax, of $72,000 at age 70. Investments within an IRA yield 7%. She would invest her after-tax distribution in tax-free municipal bonds yielding 5% if she chose averaging. Ten-year averaging yields federal income taxes of $259,370, and state income taxes on the distribution are $44,490.

As illustrated in the following table, Ms. Anderson should roll over her distribution to an IRA unless she has some pressing need for the funds. The IRA will yield $1,012,069, while averaging and investment in tax-free bonds will yield only $742,979.

Rollover

Age	Beginning balance	Income earned	Amount withdrawn	Net after taxes	Ending balance
65	$750,000	$52,500	$-0-	$-0-	$802,500
66	802,500	56,175	-0-	-0-	858,675
67	858,675	60,107	-0-	-0-	918,782
68	918,782	64,315	-0-	-0-	983,097

(*continues*)

Rollover (*continued*)

Age	Beginning balance	Income earned	Amount withdrawn	Net after taxes	Ending balance
69	983,097	68,817	-0-	-0-	1,051,914
70	1,051,914	73,634	(120,000)	72,000	1,015,548
71	1,015,548	70,388	(120,000)	72,000	955,936
72	955,936	66,619	(120,000)	72,000	902,852
73	902,852	63,200	(120,000)	72,000	846,051
74	846,051	59,224	(120,000)	72,000	785,275
75	785,275	54,969	(120,000)	72,000	720,244
76	720,244	50,417	(120,000)	72,000	650,661
77	650,661	45,546	(120,000)	72,000	576,207
78	576,207	40,335	(120,000)	72,000	496,542
80	496,542	34,758	(120,000)	72,000	411,300
81	411,300	28,791	(120,000)	72,000	320,091
82	320,091	22,406	(120,000)	72,000	222,497
83	222,497	15,575	(120,000)	72,000	118,072
84	118,072	8,265	(120,000)	72,000	6,337
85	6,337	444	(6,781)	4,069	-0-
Total				$1,012,069	

Ten-Year Averaging

Age	Beginning balance	Income earned	Amount withdrawn	Net after taxes	Ending balance
65	$446,140	$22,307	$-0-	$-0-	$468,447
66	468,447	23,422	-0-	-0-	491,869
67	491,869	24,593	-0-	-0-	516,463

			Ten-Year Averaging (*continued*)		
Age	Beginning balance	Income earned	Amount withdrawn	Net after taxes	Ending balance
68	516,463	25,823	-0-	-0-	542,286
69	542,286	27,114	-0-	-0-	569,400
70	569,400	28,470	(72,000)	72,000	525,870
71	525,870	26,294	(72,000)	72,000	480,164
72	480,164	24,008	(72,000)	72,000	432,172
73	432,172	21,609	(72,000)	72,000	381,781
74	381,781	19,089	(72,000)	72,000	328,870
75	328,870	16,443	(72,000)	72,000	273,313
76	273,313	13,666	(72,000)	72,000	214,979
77	214,979	10,749	(72,000)	72,000	153,728
78	153,728	7,686	(72,000)	72,000	89,414
79	89,414	4,471	(72,000)	72,000	21,885
80	21,885	1,094	(22,979)	22,979	-0-
Total				$742,979	

Additional Taxes

Tax on Early Distributions

Most distributions from qualified retirement plans are subject to an additional tax of 10% if the distributions occur before the individual becomes 59½ years of age. Distributions from qualified employee retirement plans under Sec. 401(k), qualified annuity plans, tax-sheltered annuity plans for employees of public school and tax-exempt organizations, and individual retirement accounts (IRA) (including Simple IRAs and Roth IRAs) are subject to this tax. The tax applies only to the portion of a distribution that is included in gross income. (See Sec. 72(t).)

Distributions from IRAs and other qualified plans are not subject to the 10% tax in the following situations:

- A distribution is made as part of a series of substantially equal periodic (at least annual) payments over an individual's life (or life expectancy) or the joint lives (or joint life expectancy) of a plan participant and beneficiary. If the distribution is from a qualified employee plan, the payments must begin after separation from service.

- A distribution is made to a beneficiary or to the estate of the plan participant or annuity holder on or after his or her death.

- A distribution is made because the plan participant is totally and permanently disabled. (See Secs. 72(q) and 72(t).)

Distributions from qualified plans other than IRAs are not subject to the 10% tax in the following situations:

- A distribution made to a plan participant after separation from service with the employer if the separation occurred during or after the calendar year in which the plan participant reached age 55

- A distribution to the extent the plan participant had deductible medical expenses (the medical expenses in excess of 7.5% of adjusted gross income)

- A distribution to alternate payees under a qualified domestic relations order

- A distribution to an individual separated from service and receiving benefits as of March 1, 1986, made under a written election designating a specific schedule of benefit payments

- A distribution made to correct excess deferrals, excess contributions, or excess aggregate contributions

- A distribution allocable to investment in a deferred annuity contract before August 14, 1982

- A distribution from an annuity contract under a qualified personal injury settlement

- A distribution from an immediate annuity contract

- A distribution under a deferred annuity contract purchased by an individual's employer upon a plan termination, if held by the employer until the individual's separation from service (see Secs. 72(q) and 72(t))

The last three exceptions apply only to deferred annuity contracts not purchased by qualified employer plans.

Distributions from IRAs are not subject to the 10% tax in the following situations:

- A distribution made after 1996, to the extent the plan participant had deductible medical expenses (the medical expenses in excess of 7.5% of adjusted gross income).

- A distribution made after 1997, if the distribution is used for qualified higher education expenses of the individual, the individual's spouse, child, or grandchild, or the spouse's child or grandchild. Qualified higher education expenses are defined as tuition at a postsecondary educational institution, books, fees, supplies, and equipment.

- A distribution made after 1996 to an unemployed individual to the extent of premiums paid during the year for medical care insurance for the individual and the individual's spouse and dependents. The individual must have been unemployed and received unemployment for 12 consecutive weeks.

- A distribution in a taxable year beginning after 1997 that is a qualified first-time home buyer distribution used to pay the qualified acquisition costs of acquiring a principal residence. The first-time homebuyer—an individual who had no present ownership interest in a principal residence during the two-year period ending on the acquisition date of the new principal residence—can be the individual receiving the distribution, or the recipient can be individual's spouse, child, grandchild, or ancestor, or the spouse's child, grandchild, or ancestor. (See Sec. 72(t).)

A penalty tax of 5% rather than 10% is due on early distributions from a deferred annuity contract if, on March 1, 1986, the participant was receiving payments under a written election providing a specific schedule for the distributions.

Required Distributions

Distributions Before Participant's Death

Generally, distributions from a qualified plan or an IRA must begin no later than April 1 of the year following the calendar year in which an individual reaches 70½ years of age. If the distribution is less than the required distribution, an excise tax is applied to the difference in the distribution made to the individual and the required distribution. The excise tax rate is 50%. (See Sec. 4974.)

The 1996 Small Business Act added an exception to the required distribution provision. After 1996, participants in qualified plans are not required to begin receiving distributions after reaching age 70½ if still employed. This exception does not apply to 5% owners and IRA owners. When the participant retires and begins taking distributions, the accrued benefit must be actuarially increased to reflect the later commencement of distributions. (See Sec. 401(a)(9)(C).)

The required payments at age 70½ can be determined based upon:

- The life of the participant

- The lives of the participant and a designated beneficiary

- A period not extending beyond the expected life of the participant

- A period not extending beyond the joint expected lives of the participant and a designated beneficiary. (See Sec. 4974(b), Sec. 401(a)(9).)

After the starting year for periodic distributions, the participant must receive the required distribution by December 31 of each year. A payment is required for the year in which the participant reaches age 70½, even though the payments may begin as late as April 1 of the following year. If the first required payment is made in that following year, another required payment must be made by December 31 of that year. (See Prop. Reg. 1.401(a)(9)-1.)

The minimum amount of the distribution is determined by dividing the amount in the participant's qualified plan or IRA by the life expectancy previously discussed. This number may be determined by using the tables in Reg. Sec. 1.72-9. The participant may elect to determine this life expectancy only once when distributions begin. If this election is not made, life expectancy is redetermined annually. If the participant elects the first option, the life expectancy determined initially is simply reduced by one each year. If the participant does not make an election and the life expectancy is redetermined annually, benefits are drawn over the participant's and spouse's actual lifetimes. However, this annual redetermination of life expectancy may result in a shorter period for the beneficiary's distributions upon the death of the participant. (See Sec. 401.)

How this election is made is not clear. Section 401 requires that it be made in the first year a distribution is required or made. The prudent approach would be to send a letter to the administrator of the pension plan or IRA, along with attaching an election to the individual's tax return.

If a nonspousal beneficiary is more than 10 years younger than the individual, the life expectancy must be determined under the minimum-distribution incidental benefit requirement. The tables to determine life expectancy under this provision are found in Prop. Reg. Sec. 1.401(a)(9)-2.

If an individual has more than one IRA, all of the IRAs must be aggregated to determine the minimum distribution. (See Sec. 408(d).) The distribution may be made from one or a combination of the IRAs. (See Notice 88-38, 1988-1 CB 524.)

Distributions After the Employee's Death

If the participant was receiving periodic distributions before his or her death, any payments not made as of the time of death must be distributed at least as rapidly as under the distribution method being used at the date of death.

If the participant dies before the required distribution date, the entire account must be distributed by either December 31 of the fifth year following the year of the participant's death, or payments must begin within one year of the participant's death and must be made in annual amounts over the life or life expectancy of the designated beneficiary. If the designated beneficiary is a surviving spouse, payments may be received over a period no longer than the life or life expectancy of the surviving spouse and the distributions must begin no later than the date on which the participant would have reached age 70½. (See Sec. 401, Prop. Reg. Sec. 1.402(a)(9)-1.)

EXAMPLE

Mr. Smith becomes 70 on August 29, Year 1. Mrs. Smith becomes 68 on January 7, Year 2. Mr. Smith has two IRAs. IRA-A has a balance of $50,000 and IRA-B has a balance of $150,000 on December 31, Year 1.

Since Mr. Smith becomes 70½ in February of Year 2, he must receive his first distribution from his IRAs no later than April 1, Year 3. Mr. and Mrs. Smiths' life expectancies are calculated using Mr. Smith's attained age as of his birthday and Mrs. Smith's attained age as of her birthday in the calendar year in which Mr. Smith attains age 70½. Mr. Smith attains age 70½ in calendar year Year 2. In Year 2 Mr. Smith becomes 71 and Mrs. Smith becomes 68. Using Table VI in Reg. Sec. 1.72-9, the ordinary joint life and last survivor life expectancy for the Smiths is 21.2. The account balances for the immediately preceding December 31 is the amount used to compute the distribution. Mr. Smith must withdraw $200,000/21.2 or $9,434 by April 1, Year 3.

Mr. Smith's second distribution must be received by December 31, Year 3. If Mr. Smith does not elect to do otherwise, the life expectancy for subsequent years will be the 21.2 years determined less 1 year for each intervening year. If Mr. Smith so elects, the life expectancy can be redetermined each year.

Tax On Excess Distributions

The tax on excess distributions was repealed by the Taxpayer Relief Act of 1997. Distributions after December 31, 1996 are not subject to the tax. Distributions in excess of $150,000 or an indexed amount in Sec. 4980A were generally subject to a 15% penalty tax. The indexed amount was $148,500 in 1994, $150,000 in 1995, and $155,000 in 1996. (See Sec. 4980A, IR 95-57.) This tax was offset by the 10% penalty tax on early distributions, if applicable.

The 15% excess distribution tax did not apply to the following:

- Distributions made after the death of the participant

- Distributions made to a spouse or former spouse under a qualified domestic relations order if the distribution was not included in the gross income of the participant

- Distributions based on the participant's investment in the contract

- Distributions rolled over tax free

- Distributions of annuity contracts to the extent not included in the participant's gross income

- Distributions of excess deferrals

- Distributions of excess contributions or excess aggregate contributions (see Sec. 4980A)

If a lump-sum distribution was received and income averaging was elected, the tax was applicable to the distribution in excess of $775,000 (5 × $155,000 – the indexed annual amount discussed above) in 1996. (See Sec. 4980A(d).)

A grandfather election was allowed when Sec. 4980A was enacted that might have reduced the distribution subject to the tax. The taxpayer had to make the election on his or her 1987 or 1988 income tax return.

Tax on Excess Accumulations

The tax on excess accumulations was repealed by the Taxpayer Relief Act of 1997. An additional 15% estate tax was imposed if an individual died with an excess retirement accumulation. (See Sec. 4980A.) None of the credits, deductions, or exclusions applicable to the estate tax could be applied against this tax. (See Sec. 4980A.) The amount subject to the tax was determined as follows.

The values of the decedent's interests in qualified retirement plans and individual retirement plans were aggregated. This amount could be reduced by:

- The value of the amount payable under a qualified domestic relations order, if includible in the income of the alternate payee

- The value of the individual's investment in the contract

- The excess of interests payable immediately after death over the value of those interests immediately before death

- Amounts rolled over by the surviving spouse into an individual retirement account established in the surviving spouse's name, an account into which no more contributions or transfers may be made

The excess of this net amount over a hypothetical annuity was subject to the tax. The hypothetical annuity was a single-life annuity calculated as if the individual had not died. The life expectancy was based on the decedent's age in whole years on the date of death. The annual payment used in computing the annuity was the greater of $150,000 or an indexed amount in Sec. 4980A. The indexed amount was $148,500 in 1994; $150,000 in 1995; and $155,000 in 1996. The factor was determined by using Table A of Regulation Sec. 20.2031-7(f).

A grandfather election was allowed when Sec. 4980A was enacted that might have reduced the accumulation subject to the tax. The taxpayer had to make the election on his or her 1987 or 1988 income tax return.

EXAMPLE

Assume the decedent was a highly compensated executive. At her death in 1996, the value of the decedent's employer plan was $1,000,000. Based on the decedent's life expectancy immediately before death and the applicable rate, the present value of an annuity paying $155,000 annually was $775,000. The excess $225,000 ($1,000,000 − $775,000) resulted in an additional tax of $33,750 ($225,000 × 15%).

Special Provisions for IRAs

Taxation of Distributions from an IRA

Since most payments into an IRA result in deductions from gross income and the income of the IRA is tax-exempt, the owner of the IRA generally has no investment in the plan and all distributions from the plan are totally taxable. However, nondeductible payments into the plan are allowed, requiring a special application of the Sec. 72 annuity rules. When a distribution is made from an IRA that has received nondeductible payments, Sec. 408(d)(2) requires that the value of the contract, the income accruing to the account, and the investment in the account be computed as of the close of that year. For this purpose, the value of the contract is increased by the amount of any distributions during the year.

EXAMPLE

Ms. Green made a $2,000 deductible payment to her IRA each year from Year 1 to Year 7, for total deductible contributions of $14,000. In each year from Year 8 to Year 12, she made a $2,000 nondeductible payment to the account, for total nondeductible contributions of $10,000. In Year 13, she withdrew $6,000. At the end of Year 13, the account had a balance of $30,000. In Year 14, she withdrew $9,000. At the end of Year 14, the account had a balance of $22,000. The portion of Ms. Green's distributions treated as a nontaxable return of capital is computed as follows:

(continues)

Year 13 $\quad \dfrac{\$10,000}{\$30,000 + \$6,000} \times \$6,000 = \$1,667$

Year 14 $\quad \dfrac{\$10,000 - \$1,667}{\$22,000 + \$9,000} \times \$9,000 = \$2,419$

In Year 14, the investment in the contract (the nondeductible contributions) must be reduced by the excludable portion of prior distributions—in this case the $1,667 excluded in Year 13.

Generally No More Contributions to IRAs After Age 70½

Individuals may not make contributions to an IRA beginning in the year the individual reaches age 70½. (See Sec. 219(d)(1).) However, see the discussion of Roth IRAs that follows.

Not Eligible for 5- or 10-Year Averaging

IRA distributions are not eligible for 5- or 10-year averaging. (See Sec. 402.)

Inherited IRAs

For individuals other than a surviving spouse, distributions from an inherited IRA cannot be rolled over. No deductible contributions can be made to an inherited IRA. (See Secs. 219 and 408.) Distributions from inherited IRAs and qualified plans are income to beneficiary. There is no step-up in basis to the value of the account at death. (See Sec. 1014(b)(9)(A).)

Roth IRAs

The Tax Relief Act of 1997 (followed by several technical corrections in the IRS Restructuring and Reform Act of 1998) established a new type of IRA referred to as a *Roth IRA*. Contributions to a Roth IRA are not deductible, but distributions are not included in gross income if the requirements are met.

Contributions

Generally, the conditions for regular IRAs apply to Roth IRAs. For example, the individual making the contribution must have earned income equal to $2,000 or the amount contributed, if less. The contributions result in no immediate tax benefits because there is no deduction for contributions to a Roth IRA. Unlike regular IRAs, contributions to a Roth IRA are allowed after age 70½.

Contributions to all IRAs are limited to $2,000 annually. The amount that can be contributed to a Roth IRA is phased out for single taxpayers with adjusted gross income between $95,000 and $110,000; for married taxpayers filing jointly with adjusted gross income between $150,000 and $160,000; and for married taxpayers filing separately with adjusted gross income between $0 and $10,000. (See Sec. 408A(c)(3)(A).)

Individuals can also make contributions to spousal Roth IRAs.

Distributions

Distributions from a Roth IRA are not included in gross income and are not subject to the 10% early withdrawal penalty if contributions to the IRA are held in the IRA for five years and one of the following conditions are met when a distribution is made:

- The individual has attained age 59½.

- The distribution is made to a beneficiary (or the individual's estate) on or after the individual's death.

- The individual has become disabled.

- The distribution is for qualified first-time home buyer expenses. (See Sec. 408A(d).)

Conversion from an Ordinary IRA to a Roth IRA

Ordinary IRAs can be rolled over into a Roth IRA if the taxpayer's adjusted gross income does not exceed $100,000 and the taxpayer is not married filing separately. (See Sec. 408A(d)(3).) For years beginning after December 31, 2004, required distributions from ordinary IRAs will not be included in adjusted gross income in determining whether the $100,000 limit is exceeded. For years before 2005, required distributions from ordinary IRAs are included in adjusted gross income for this purpose. (See Sec. 408A(c)(3).)

Potentially taxable amounts that are rolled over into the Roth IRA must be included in gross income of the individual. If the rollover was made before 1999, the amount rolled over could be included in gross income ratably over four years, lessening the burden of paying the taxes. An individual could elect out of the four-year recognition of income, allowing all of the income to be included in 1998 if it was advantageous to do so. The election was irrevocable and cannot be changed after the due date (including extensions) for the return for the first year the income is included in gross income. (See Sec. 408A(d)(3)(A)(iii).)

If an individual makes a conversion to a Roth IRA, recognizing the income over the four-year period, and dies during the four-year period, any amounts remaining to be included must be included on the final return of the deceased individual. The remaining amounts can be included in the income of the surviving spouse over the original deferral period if the surviving spouse is the sole beneficiary of the Roth IRA and makes an irrevocable election to do so. (See Sec. 408A(d)(3)(E)(ii).)

Distributions after Conversion from an Ordinary IRA to a Roth IRA

If a conversion occurred before 1999 and income is being recognized over a period of four years, distributions before the four-year period has passed (before 2001) will result in the acceleration of the lesser of the following amounts:

- The taxable amount of the withdrawal as determined under the ordering rules that follow (the amount of the distribution, unless the IRA contains both conversion amounts and other contributions)
- The remaining taxable amount of the conversion

This is in addition to the scheduled recognition of income from the conversion—that year's one-fourth of the converted amount. (See Sec. 408A(d)(3)(E)(i).)

If a Roth IRA contains amounts from a conversion and from other contributions, Sec. 408A(d)(4)(A) provides ordering rules for distributions. A distribution is treated as made first from regular Roth contributions. Amounts distributed in excess of contributions are considered to be from the earliest converted amounts.

Planning with Roth IRAs

Individuals should consider starting a Roth IRA, even with a small amount, as soon as possible to start the running of the five-year time period. A contribution made by April 15 can be designated as made for the last taxable year. The five-year holding period previously discussed under "Distributions" begins with the year for which a contribution is first made to a Roth IRA. Subsequent contributions or conversions do not start new five-year holding periods. (See Sec. 408A(d)(2)(B).)

Roth IRAs present an attractive estate-planning alternative. Unlike with an ordinary IRA, the individual accumulating retirement benefits in a Roth IRA does not have to make withdrawals from the Roth IRA after reaching age 70½. In addition, ordinary IRAs result in taxable income to the beneficiaries. Distributions from a Roth IRA, if distributed after the five-year period, will not result in taxable income to the beneficiaries. This effect of this difference from ordinary IRAs could be important. The taxes due upon the death of a person owning primarily an ordinary IRA could be larger than one would expect. The example that follows under "Roth IRA or Ordinary IRA" illustrates the difference.

Roth IRA or Ordinary IRA

If an individual continues to generate at least $2,000 of earned income annually, a Roth IRA should be seriously considered.

COMPUTATION AID: For a worksheet to be used to compare the relative performance of a Roth IRA to an ordinary IRA, see Worksheet 2.5 on page 58.

The following example illustrates the relative performance of an ordinary IRA and a Roth IRA.

EXAMPLE

Assume that Ms. Wilson, age 50, invests $2,000 annually in a Roth IRA. She earns income of 10% on the assets in the IRA and her marginal tax rate is 31%. After making contributions for 10 years, she begins making withdrawals at age 60. Her marginal tax rate drops to 28%. She can withdraw $5,188 each year for 10 years, paying no taxes.

Roth IRA

Annual contribution	Interest	End-of-year balance	Net withdrawal
$2,000	$200	$2,200	
2,000	420	4,620	
2,000	662	7,282	
2,000	928	10,210	
2,000	1,221	13,431	
2,000	1,543	16,974	
2,000	1,897	20,872	
2,000	2,287	25,159	
2,000	2,716	29,875	
2,000	3,187	35,062	
−5,188	2,987	32,862	$5,188
−5,188	2,767	30,441	5,188
−5,188	2,525	27,778	5,188
−5,188	2,259	24,850	5,188
−5,188	1,966	21,628	5,188
−5,188	1,644	18,084	5,188
−5,188	1,290	14,185	5,188

Roth IRA (continued)			
Annual contribution	**Interest**	**End-of-year balance**	**Net withdrawal**
−5,188	900	9,897	5,188
−5,188	471	5,180	5,188
−5,180			5,180

In comparison, if she had invested in an ordinary IRA, her net withdrawal, after taxes, is only $3,735:

Ordinary IRA				
Annual contribution	**Interest**	**End-of-year balance**	**Taxes**	**Net withdrawal**
$2,000	$200	$2,200		
2,000	420	4,620		
2,000	662	7,282		
2,000	928	10,210		
2,000	1,221	13,431		
2,000	1,543	16,974		
2,000	1,897	20,872		
2,000	2,287	25,159		
2,000	2,716	29,875		
2,000	3,187	35,062		
−5,188	2,987	32,862	−$1,453	$3,735
−5,188	2,767	30,441	−1,453	3,735
−5,188	2,525	27,778	−1,453	3,735
−5,188	2,259	24,850	−1,453	3,735
−5,188	1,966	21,628	−1,453	3,735

(*continues*)

Ordinary IRA (*continued*)

Annual contribution	Interest	End-of-year balance	Taxes	Net withdrawal
−5,188	1,644	18,084	−1,453	3,735
−5,188	1,290	14,185	−1,453	3,735
−5,188	900	9,897	−1,453	3,735
−5,188	471	5,180	−1,453	3,735
−5,180			−1,450	3,730

In order to consider the most optimistic view of the ordinary IRA, assume that Ms. Wilson is well-disciplined and carefully saves her tax savings each year. Assume that she deposits the $620 tax savings from the ordinary IRA contributions into her savings account, earning 5% annually. She can make a net withdrawal of $876 annually, making the total annual withdrawals available for her use $4,611:

Savings Account

Tax savings	Interest	Taxes	End-of-year balance	Net withdrawal
$620	$31	−$10	$ 641	
620	63	−20	1,305	
620	96	−30	1,991	
620	131	−40	2,701	
620	166	−51	3,436	
620	203	−63	4,196	
620	241	−75	4,982	
620	280	−87	5,795	
620	321	−99	6,637	
620	363	−112	7,507	
−876	332	−93	6,870	$876

Savings Account (*continued*)				
Tax savings	Interest	Taxes	End-of-year balance	Net withdrawal
−876	300	−84	6,210	876
−876	267	−75	5,526	876
−876	232	−65	4,817	876
−876	197	−55	4,083	876
−876	160	−45	3,322	876
−876	122	−34	2,534	876
−876	83	−23	1,718	876
−876	42	−12	872	876
−872				872

Good planning would require a similar analysis based on an individual's expected tax rates and growth rates. In many situations, a Roth IRA would appear to be a wise investment.

A similar analysis should be made for the decision to convert an ordinary IRA into a Roth IRA. If the individual has no other source of funds to pay the taxes on the conversion, the cost of removing the necessary funds from the IRA to pay the taxes is heavy. In addition to the income taxes due, the withdrawal will be subject to the early withdrawal penalty. If the taxes can be withdrawn from some other source currently producing little income and the funds will be left in the Roth IRA for a long period of time, the conversion might make sense.

COMPUTATION AID: To analyze the conversion of an ordinary IRA to a Roth IRA, see Worksheet 2.5 on page 58. Use the "Savings Account" worksheet to compute the cost of removing funds from another source to pay the taxes.

However, the estate-planning potential of Roth IRAs should also be considered. The following example illustrates the estate tax consequences of converting an ordinary IRA into a Roth IRA.

EXAMPLE

Upon his death, Mr. Brown owns an ordinary IRA worth $1,000,000 and his net estate is valued at $2,000,000. His only living relative is his nephew. Mr. Brown was not making required distributions from his IRA before his death. Since the beneficiary of his IRA is his nephew, the entire IRA must be distributed within five years. Assume that the date of death is in 2006 so that the applicable exemption amount is $1,000,000. Also assume that both Mr. Brown's and the nephew's marginal income tax rate is 39.6%. The taxes due within a short time after Mr. Brown's death are:

Net estate before taxes	$2,000,000
Estate taxes ($780,800 – $345,800)	$435,000
Income taxes ($1,000,000 × 39.6%)	$396,000
Total taxes	$831,000
Net estate after taxes	$1,169,000

If the IRA were a Roth IRA, the taxes due would only be the estate taxes. The net estate should also be somewhat smaller. To illustrate, assume that Mr. Brown had converted his IRA into a Roth IRA in 2001; that his investments grow at a constant rate of 10% for the next five years before his death; and that assets outside of the IRA are used to pay the income taxes due upon conversion. The value of the estate in 2001 and net estate after taxes would be:

Value of IRA in 2001, with 10% discount factor	$620,921
Value of other investments in 2001, with 10% discount factor	$620,921
Total assets in 2001, with 10% discount factor	$1,241,842
Income tax on conversion of IRA ($620,921 × 39.6%)	$245,885
Total assets after conversion and payment of tax	$998,957
Net estate five years later (in 2006)	$1,604,000

Estate taxes ($602,600 − $345,800)	$256,800
Net estate after taxes	$1,347,200

The larger net estate results because the income taxes paid upon the conversion reduce the net estate subject to estate tax, and the growth in the Roth IRA escapes income taxation.

Withholding on Distributions

Periodic Payments

Income taxes must generally be withheld from periodic payments from a qualified plan or IRA as if the payments were wages of an employee. The participant may elect to not have any amounts withheld. (See Sec. 3405(a).)

Nonperiodic Distributions

For any distribution that is neither a periodic payment nor a distribution eligible for rollover treatment, 10% of the distribution must be withheld. The participant may elect to not have any amounts withheld. (See Sec. 3405(b).)

Distributions Eligible for Rollover Treatment

For any distribution that is eligible for rollover treatment, 20% of the distribution must be withheld. Withholding is not required if the distribution is paid directly to another qualified plan or to an IRA. (See Sec. 3405(c).)

CHAPTER 2 COMPUTATION AIDS

Worksheet 2.1 Computation Aid Pension 1

Computing Excluded Portion of an Annuity
(Annuity starting date before November 19, 1996)

(Not for annuities where an election under Reg. Sec. 1.72 has been made to use the gender-specific tables.)

$$\text{Exclusion ratio} = \frac{\text{investment in contract}}{\text{expected return}} = \frac{\qquad}{\qquad} = \underline{\qquad}$$

$$\text{Excluded portion of annuity} = \frac{\qquad}{\text{payment}} \times \frac{\qquad}{\text{exclusion ratio}} = \underline{\qquad}$$

Computation of expected return:

Periodic payment	_____
Multiply by	×
Number of payments per year*	_____
Multiply by	×
Number of periods in years†	_____
Equals: Expected return	_____

---

*Generally 12 payments per year
†For fixed-period annuities, the number of periods specified in the contract. For annuities payable for life, the factor determined by using Reg. Sec. 1.72-9. If the annuity starting date is after November 18, 1996, see Computation Aid Pension 2

Worksheet 2.2　Computation Aid Pension 2

Computing Excluded Portion of an Annuity
(Simplified method—annuity starting date after November 18, 1996)

$$\text{Excluded portion of each payment} = \frac{\text{investment in contract}}{\text{anticipated payments}} = \text{———}$$

For annuity starting dates after December 31, 1997,
Sec. 72(d) provides two tables for determining the anticipated payments.

If the annuity is payable over the life of a single individual,
the anticipated payments are determined as follows:

If the age of the annuitant on the annuity starting date is:	*The number of anticipated payments is:*
Not more than 55	360
More than 55 but not more than 60	310
More than 60 but not more than 65	260
More than 65 but not more than 70	210
More than 70	160

If the annuity is payable over the lives of more than one individual,
the anticipated payments are determined as follows:

If the combined ages of annuitants are:	*The number of anticipated payments is:*
Not more than 110	410
More than 110 but not more than 120	360
More than 120 but not more than 130	310
More than 130 but not more than 140	260
More than 140	210

For annuity starting dates before January 1, 1998, refer to the text for tables to determine
the number of anticipated payments.

Worksheet 2.3   Computation Aid Pension 3

Computing Taxes on Lump-Sum Distribution

Total distribution   _____

Less: Amount attributable to nondeductible contributions   _____

Less: Amount attributable to participation prior to 1974   _____

Equals: Ordinary income portion of distribution   _____

Less: Minimum distribution allowance: _____

    Lesser of:

    Ordinary income portion × 50%   _____

    or, $10,000   _____

    Reduced by:

    Ordinary income portion × 20%   _____

    Less: $20,000   _____   _____

Amount subject to averaging   =============

Five-year averaging (applicable only to years ending before 2000)

Amount subject to averaging   _____

Divide by: 5

One-fifth (20%) of ordinary income portion   =============

Worksheet 2.3   Computation Aid Pension 3 (*continued*)

Tax using 1998 or 1999 single rates   _____

Multiply by: 5

Tax using 5-year averaging   ==========

Ten-year averaging

Amount subject to averaging   _____

Divide by: 10

One-tenth (10%) of ordinary income portion   ==========

Tax using 1986 single rates   _____

Multiply by: 10

Tax using 10-year averaging   ==========

Total Tax

Lesser of 5-year averaging and 10-year averaging   _____

Add: Capital gain tax – amount attributable to participation
prior to 1974 × 20% = _____ × 20%   _____

Add: Tax on minimum distribution allowance using current
marginal rate = _____ × _____%   _____

Total tax on lump-sum distribution   ==========

Worksheet 2.4 Computation Aid Pension 4

Comparison of Rollover and Lump-Sum Distribution

Rollover—initial beginning balance equals total distribution

Age	Beginning balance	Income earned	Amount withdrawn	Net after taxes	Ending balance
Total					

Worksheet 2.4   Computation Aid Pension 4 (*continued*)

Ten-Year Averaging—Beginning balance equals distribution less taxes

Age	Beginning balance	Income earned	Amount withdrawn	Net after taxes	Ending balance
Total					

Worksheet 2.5 Computation Aid Pension 5

Comparison of Roth IRA and Ordinary IRA

Roth IRA

Annual contribution	Interest	End-of-year balance	Net withdrawal

Worksheet 2.5　Computation Aid Pension 5 (*continued*)

Ordinary IRA

Annual contribution	Interest	End-of-year balance	Taxes	Net withdrawal

Net withdrawal—ordinary IRA　　　　　　　　　　_____

Net withdrawal—savings account　　　　　　　　_____

Total available for use　　　　　　　　　　　　_____

(*continues*)

Worksheet 2.5   Computation Aid Pension 5 (*continued*)

Savings Account for Tax Savings for
Ordinary IRA Contributions

Tax savings	Interest	Taxes	End-of-year balance	Net withdrawal

Social Security Benefits

Most working Americans have been paying into the Social Security system for many years. There are at least two aspects of Social Security benefits that will directly affect most taxpayers in their retirement years. First, the individual, after proper application, will receive monthly benefits starting at age 62 or later. Second, the benefits may be partially taxable.

Social Security Retirement Benefits

In order to do effective planning for a client's retirement years, the tax advisor should have at least a basic understanding of the benefits available under Title II of the Social Security Act. Old-age, survivors, or disability insurance benefits are the benefits paid to workers, their spouses, children and parents, and to widows, widowers, and divorced persons.

Determination of Coverage

A worker's right to benefits depends upon the number of *quarters of coverage* acquired. Quarters of coverage generally are earned by performing work that produces taxable wages or self-employment income under the Social Security Act. The specific minimum requirements for a quarter of coverage depend on the date the work was performed. (See Soc. Sec. Act Sec. 213(a).)

For years before 1978, a quarter of coverage was earned for any calendar quarter in which the individual earned taxable wages of $50 or more or self-employment income of $100 or more. The amount is $100 for agricultural labor after 1954. The worker must also have self-employment income of $400 for a taxable year for years after 1950.

For 1978, a worker is given credit for one quarter for each $250 of taxable wages earned in that year, with a maximum of four quarters. Beginning in that year, taxable wages and self-employment income are added together and credit is given based on the sum. A worker must have at least $400 of self-employment income before any quarters of credit are given for self-employment income.

For years after 1978, the minimum amount of combined taxable wages and self-employment income increases each year to reflect the increase in average wages. Self-employed individuals must still have at least $400 of self-employment income in a taxable year. (See *Soc. Sec. Handbook,* SSA Pub. No. 65-008, 1997, Sec. 212; 60 *Federal Register* 54751; 61 *Federal Register* 55346; 62 *Federal Register* 58762.) For the amounts, see Table 3.1.

For most benefits, the worker must be "fully insured" by having credit for enough quarters of coverage based on age or date of death. A worker with 40 quarters of coverage is fully insured for life. (See Soc. Sec. Act Sec. 214(a).)

If a worker is fully insured, the worker and his or her family are entitled to the following benefits:

- Old-age benefits for the worker if the worker is age 62 or older.

- Disability benefits for the worker under age 65 if the worker would have been fully insured had he or she attained age 62 and has 20 quarters of coverage out of the 40 calendar quarters ending with the quarter in which the disability began.

TABLE 3.1 **Combined Taxable Wages and Self-Employed Income**

1979	$260
1980	290
1981	310
1982	340
1983	370
1984	390
1985	410
1986	440
1987	460
1988	470
1989	500
1990	520
1991	540
1992	570
1993	590
1994	620
1995	630
1996	640
1997	670
1998	700
1999	740

There are special provisions for workers disabled before the age of 31.

■ The spouse of an insured worker is entitled to retirement or disability benefits if the spouse is age 62 or over or caring for a child who is under age 16 or disabled and entitled to benefits.

■ A dependent, unmarried child of an insured worker is entitled to benefits if the child is under age 18, age 18 or over and qualified as a full-time student, or age 18 or over and under a disability that began before the child reached age 22.

- A widow or widower of a fully insured worker is entitled to benefits if age 60 or over, if caring for a child entitled to benefits if the child is under age 16 or disabled, or if the widow or widower is age 50 or over but under age 60, is disabled, and whose disability began within a certain period.

- The dependent, unmarried child of a deceased, fully insured worker is entitled to benefits if the child is under age 18, age 18 or over and qualified as a full-time student, or age 18 or over and under a disability that began before age 22.

- The dependent parents of a deceased, fully insured worker are entitled to benefits if age 62 or over.

- The divorced spouse of the worker is entitled to benefits if the couple was married for 10 years or more.

Amount of Benefits–Primary Insurance Amount

In general, an individual's Social Security benefit is based on the worker's earnings averaged over his or her working lifetime. Greatly simplified, the benefit is determined in these four steps:

- *Step 1.* Determine the number of years of earnings to use as a base.

- *Step 2.* Adjust these earnings for inflation.

- *Step 3.* Determine the average adjusted monthly earnings, based on the number of years determined in Step 1.

- *Step 4.* Multiply the average adjusted earnings by percentages in a formula that is specified by law, resulting in primary insurance amount.

A different method based on a worker's actual average monthly wage applies to most persons who became eligible for Social Security benefits before 1984.

Individuals who have not worked long enough to receive Social Security retirement benefits or who receive only a small amount may be eligible for Supplemental Security Income.

Determine the Number of Years of Earnings

Three numbers related to years are required in determining benefits. (See Soc. Sec. Act Sec. 215.)

Elapsed years are generally the number of calendar years after the year of attaining age 21 and prior to the year of attaining age 62. Special rules apply for workers born before 1930 and for male workers who attained age 62 before 1975. For survivor's benefits, elapsed years is the number of years after 1950 (or, if later, the year age 21 was attained) and the year before the worker died, but if the worker died after retirement age, use the general computation amount previously described. Special rules apply for disability benefits.

Computation base years are years in which the worker had earnings after 1950 and before the earlier of the year in which the worker became entitled for retirement or disability benefits or died. Special rules apply if periods of disability occurred during those years.

Benefit computation years are generally the number of elapsed years minus 5. Special rules apply for workers with less than two computation years and for younger disabled workers. The benefit computation years selected for the computation are the base years in which earnings were the highest.

Only wages up to maximum amounts can be considered. For years after 1950, self-employment income is included in these amounts. (See *Soc. Sec. Handbook,* SSA Pub. No. 65-008, 1997, Sec. 714; 62 *Federal Register* 58762.) These maximums are listed in Table 3.2.

Adjust These Earnings for Inflation

For workers becoming eligible after 1983, the worker's actual wages are indexed for inflation. These earnings in each year

TABLE 3.2 Maximum Wages

1937–1950	$3,000
1951–1954	3,600
1955–1958	4,200
1959–1965	4,800
1966–1967	6,600
1968–1971	7,800
1972	9,000
1973	10,800
1974	13,200
1975	14,100
1976	15,300
1977	16,500
1978	17,700
1979	22,900
1980	25,900
1981	29,700
1982	32,400
1983	35,700
1984	37,800
1985	39,600
1986	42,000
1987	43,800
1988	45,000
1989	48,000
1990	51,300
1991	53,400
1992	55,500
1993	57,600
1994	60,600
1995	61,200
1996	62,700
1997	65,400
1998	68,400
1999	72,600

after 1950 until the second year before the worker reaches age 62 are indexed. This is done by multiplying the actual earnings by the average of total wages reported by all U.S. workers in the second year before the worker reaches age 62, becomes disabled, or dies, divided by the average wages from the year being indexed. This amount is computed for all of the base years, except that for years after the indexing year (generally starting two years before age 62) the actual amount of reported earnings is used. (See Soc. Sec. Act Sec. 215.)

Table 3.3 lists the average earnings of all U.S. workers. This table would be used for an individual reaching age 62 in 1999. (See 20 C.F.R. Part 404, Subpart C, Appendix I; 60 *Federal Register* 54751; 61 *Federal Register* 55346; 62 *Federal Register* 58762.)

Determine the Average Adjusted Monthly Earnings

The indexed earnings for the benefit computation years are summed, using the years in which the indexed earnings are the greatest. The sum is divided by the number of months in these years to arrive at the worker's average indexed monthly earnings (AIME).

Multiply the Average Adjusted Earnings by Percentages in Formula

For workers reaching age 62 after 1983, the average indexed monthly earnings are multiplied by a primary insurance amount formula. (See Soc. Sec. Act Sec. 215; 62 *Federal Register* 58765.) For a worker reaching age 62 in 1999, the formula is:

90% of first $505 or less of AIME, plus

32% of any AIME above $505 to $3,043, plus

15% of any AIME above $3,043

The sum is rounded down to tenths of a dollar.

Special Minimum Primary Insurance Amount

A special minimum primary insurance amount computation is available for workers with a long history of low earnings. How-

TABLE 3.3 Average Earnings

Average of Total Wages	
Year	Average earnings
1951	$2,799.16
1952	2,973.32
1953	3,139.44
1954	3,155.64
1955	3,301.44
1956	3,532.36
1957	3,641.72
1958	3,673.80
1959	3,855.80
1960	4,007.12
1961	4,086.76
1962	4,291.40
1963	4,396.64
1964	4,576.32
1965	4,658.72
1966	4,938.36
1967	5,213.44
1968	5,571.76
1969	5,893.76
1970	6,186.24
1971	6,497.08
1972	7,133.80
1973	7,580.16
1974	8,030.76
1975	8,630.92
1976	9,226.48

TABLE 3.3 Average Earnings (*continued*)

Average of Total Wages

Year	Average earnings
1977	9,779.44
1978	10,556.03
1979	11,479.46
1980	12,513.46
1981	13,773.10
1982	14,531.34
1983	15,239.24
1984	16,135.07
1985	16,822.51
1986	17,321.82
1987	18,426.51
1988	19,334.04
1989	20,099.55
1990	21,027.98
1991	21,811.60
1992	22,935.42
1993	23,132.67
1994	23,753.53
1995	24,705.66
1996	25,913.90
1997	27,426.00

ever, the formula previously outlined is usually more advantageous. (See Soc. Sec. Act Sec. 215.)

COMPUTATION AID: For a worksheet to compute the primary insurance amount, see Worksheet 3.1 on page 91.

EXAMPLE

Mr. Jones reaches age 62 in January 1999, retires, and promptly files the necessary forms to become entitled to retirement benefits. He began working in 1954 at age 17 and has had earnings in excess of the FICA wage base every year since he began working.

Mr. Jones's elapsed years are 40, the number of calendar years after the year of attainment of age 21 and prior to the year of attainment of age 62. His computation base years are 1954 through 1998, the years in which he had earnings after 1950 and before the year in which he became entitled for retirement. His benefit computation years are determined in the table that follows. The number of benefit computation years are generally the number of elapsed years minus 5 (or 40 minus 5, equaling 35).

To determine indexed earnings for each of the computation years, each year's actual earnings, limited to the maximum amount for that year, are multiplied by the ratio of average annual wages in 1997 (two years prior to Mr. Jones's retirement) to the average annual wages in the year being determined. For example, to determine Mr. Jones's indexed earnings for 1954, multiply his actual earnings from 1954 limited to $3,600 by the ratio of average annual wages in 1997 ($27,426) to average annual wages in 1954 ($3,156).

$$\$3,600 \times \frac{\$27,426}{\$3,155.64} = \$31,288$$

As required, for the two years prior to Mr. Jones's retirement, his actual earnings, limited to the maximums for those years, are used rather than indexed earnings amounts.

The 35 computation years with the highest indexed earnings are the benefit computation years. Consequently, indexed earnings for 1954, 1956–1958, and 1960–1965 are excluded from the computation.

Computation Years

Year	Age	Maximum income	Average of total wages	Computed AIME	Not included	Benefit computation years
1954	17	$ 3,600	$ 3,155.64	$ 31,288	$ 31,288	0
1955	18	4,200	3,301.44	34,891		$ 34,891

Computation Years (*continued*)

Year	Age	Maximum income	Average of total wages	Computed AIME	Not included	Benefit computation years
1956	19	4,200	3,532.36	32,610	32,610	0
1957	20	4,200	3,641.72	31,630	31,630	0
1958	21	4,200	3,673.80	31,354	31,354	0
1959	22	4,800	3,855.88	34,142		34,142
1960	23	4,800	4,007.12	32,853	32,853	0
1961	24	4,800	4,086.76	32,213	32,213	0
1962	25	4,800	4,291.40	30,676	30,676	0
1963	26	4,800	4,396.64	29,942	29,942	0
1964	27	4,800	4,576.32	28,767	28,767	0
1965	28	4,800	4,658.72	28,258	28,258	0
1966	29	6,600	4,938.36	36,654		36,654
1967	30	6,600	5,213.44	34,720		34,720
1968	31	7,800	5,571.76	38,394		38,394
1969	32	7,800	5,893.76	36,296		36,296
1970	33	7,800	6,186.24	34,580		34,580
1971	34	7,800	6,497.08	32,926		32,926
1972	35	9,000	7,133.80	34,601		34,601
1973	36	10,800	7,580.16	39,076		39,076
1974	37	13,200	8,030.76	45,080		45,080
1975	38	14,100	8,630.92	44,805		44,805
1976	39	15,300	9,226.48	45,480		45,480
1977	40	16,500	9,779.44	46,274		46,274
1978	41	17,700	10,556.03	45,987		45,987
1979	42	22,900	11,479.46	54,711		54,711
1980	43	25,900	12,513.46	56,766		56,766
1981	44	29,700	13,773.10	59,141		59,141
1982	45	32,400	14,531.34	61,151		61,151
1983	46	35,700	15,239.24	64,249		64,249

(*continues*)

Computation Years (*continued*)

Year	Age	Maximum income	Average of total wages	Computed AIME	Not included	Benefit computation years
1984	47	37,800	16,135.07	64,252		64,252
1985	48	39,600	16,822.51	64,560		64,560
1986	49	42,000	17,321.82	66,499		66,499
1987	50	43,800	18,426.51	65,192		65,192
1988	51	45,000	19,334.04	63,834		63,834
1989	52	48,000	20,099.55	65,496		65,496
1990	53	51,300	21,027.98	66,909		66,909
1991	54	53,400	21,811.60	67,145		67,145
1992	55	55,500	22,935.42	66,366		66,366
1993	56	57,600	23,132.67	68,290		68,290
1994	57	60,600	23,753.53	69,969		69,969
1995	58	61,200	24,705.66	67,939		67,939
1996	59	62,700	25,913.90	66,359		66,359
1997	60	65,400	27,426.00	65,400		65,400
1998	61	68,400		68,400		68,400
1999	62	72,600				NA
						$1,808,133

The sum of the indexed earnings amounts for the benefit computation years is $1,808,133. This sum is divided by the number of months in the 35 years ($12 \times 35 = 420$) to arrive at Mr. Jones's average indexed monthly earnings (AIME) of $4,305.

Mr. Jones's primary insurance amount is determined by applying the 1999 formula to his AIME of $4,305.

90% of $505	$ 455
32% of ($3,043 − $505)	812
15% of ($4,305 − $3,043)	189
Primary Insurance Amount	$1,456

Since Mr. Jones is retiring at age 62, the earliest possible date to become eligible for retirement benefits, his primary insurance amount will be reduced by 20%, as will be discussed later. Consequently, his monthly benefit will be $1,456 × 80% = $1,165. This amount should be adjusted yearly due to cost-of-living increases in benefits.

Computation of 1999 Primary Insurance Amounts for Selected AIMEs

AIME of $3,000
90% of $505	$ 455
32% of ($3,000 − $505)	798
Primary Insurance Amount	$1,253

AIME of $2,500
90% of $505	$ 455
32% of ($2,500 − $505)	638
Primary Insurance Amount	$1,093

AIME of $2,000
90% of $505	$ 455
32% of ($2,000 − $505)	478
Primary Insurance Amount	$ 933

AIME of $1,500
90% of $505	$ 455
32% of ($1,500 − $505)	318
Primary Insurance Amount	$ 773

AIME of $1,000
90% of $505	$ 455
32% of ($1,000 − $505)	158
Primary Insurance Amount	$ 613

Worker and Family Benefits

Worker Benefits

A worker is entitled to his or her primary insurance amount each month if he or she elects to begin drawing benefits at age 65. The worker must be fully insured, be at least 65 years of age, and must file an application. Cost-of-living increases are automatic, based upon increases in the Consumer Price Index. (See Soc. Sec. Act Sec. 215.)

The retirement age of 65 is scheduled to increase. The full retirement age will be 66 for workers reaching age 62 in 2005, and 67 for workers reaching age 62 in 2022. These changes will be phased in at the rate of 2 months per year beginning in 1999 for the age 66 and beginning in 2017 for age 67. (See Soc. Sec. Act Sec. 202.)

The monthly benefit is reduced if the worker elects to begin drawing benefits prior to age 65. Early retirement benefits can be claimed as early as age 62. Age 62 will continue to be the early retirement age when the full retirement age is increased. The monthly benefit is reduced by $\frac{5}{9}$ of 1% of the primary insurance amount for each month prior to age 65. Early retirement at age 62 will result in the reduction of the monthly benefit of $\frac{5}{9} \times 1\% \times 36$ months $= 20\%$. This formula will be adjusted when the full retirement age increases. The reduction in benefits will continue as long as the worker continues to receive benefits. (See Soc. Sec. Act Sec. 202.)

A worker electing to delay drawing benefits beyond age 65 will receive a credit increasing his or her monthly benefits. The amount of the credit depends on the year the worker becomes age 65. For workers who become age 65 after 1989, the delayed retirement credit is $\frac{1}{4}$ of 1% plus $\frac{1}{24}$ of 1% for each even-numbered year through 2008. After becoming fully phased in, the credit will be 8% per year. The credit for a worker reaching age 65 in 1998 or 1999 is 5.5%. A worker reaching age 65 in 1998 or 1999 and deferring retirement until after age 70 will receive a monthly benefit 27.5% (5 years $\times$ 5.5%) larger than the monthly benefit that would be received with retirement at age 65. (See Soc. Sec. Act Sec. 202.)

A worker can apply for benefits and continue to work. However, there may be reductions in benefits. Benefits may be reduced if the worker has excess earnings. Wages and self-employment income are combined to determine earnings for this purpose. Excess earnings are defined (in 1999) as earnings in excess of $9,600 ($800 per month) for workers under age 65 and $15,500 ($1,292 per month) for workers age 65 through 69. The minimum amounts of earnings for workers under age 65 will continue to increase whenever there is a cost-of-living increase in benefits. Minimum amounts of earnings for workers age 65 through 69 are scheduled to be $17,000 in 2000, $25,000 in 2001, and $30,000 in 2002. (See Soc. Sec. Act Sec. 203; 62 *Federal Register* 58762.)

The reduction in benefits is equal to one-half of excess earnings for workers under age 65 and one-third of excess earnings for workers age 65 to age 69. Workers 70 years of age or more may have any amount of earnings with no reduction in benefits. The reduction is computed on an annual basis, except for one grace year when it may be computed on a monthly basis after the worker becomes entitled to benefits. If the amount determined is not a multiple of $10, it is rounded to the nearest multiple of $10.

EXAMPLE

Ms. Smith, age 63, retired in 1998 and is receiving a monthly retirement benefit, based upon her own primary insurance amount, of $800. During 1999, Ms. Smith earns $18,000 at a part-time job. Her annual benefits of $9,600 ($800 × 12) will be reduced by $4,200.

$$\frac{\$18,000 - \$9,600}{2} = \$4,200$$

If Ms. Smith were age 66, her annual benefits would be reduced by $830.

$$\frac{\$18,000 - \$15,500}{3} = \$833, \text{ rounded to } \$830$$

Spouse's Benefits

The spouse of a worker entitled to benefits is also entitled to benefits if the spouse has filed an application, is at least age 62 or is caring for a child eligible for benefits, and whose own primary insurance amount is less than one-half of the worker's primary insurance amount. The spouse's full monthly benefit at age 65 would be half of the primary insurance amount of the worker. Spouse's benefits are generally reduced if payments begin before age 65. This reduction is 0.69% for each month prior to age 65, with a maximum reduction of 25%. There is no reduction if the spouse is caring for a covered child. Benefits may also be reduced if either spouse has excess earnings. (See Soc. Sec. Act Sec. 202.)

EXAMPLE

Mr. Brown retires at age 62 with a primary insurance amount of $1,251. His benefit is reduced by 20%, to $1,001, due to his early retirement.

Mr. and Ms. Brown have been married for 40 years. Ms. Brown has not worked outside the home and has no earnings record. Upon application at age 62, she is entitled to a monthly benefit of $626 (50% of $1,251), reduced by 25% due to early retirement. Her reduced benefit is $470 ($626 × 75%).

Divorced Spouses

The divorced spouse of a worker may be entitled to benefits if the worker is entitled to benefits or if the divorce has been final for at least two continuous years. If the divorced spouse first applies for benefits after becoming age 65, the benefit will be equal to one-half of the worker's age 65 benefit. Between ages 62 and 65, the benefit is reduced by 0.69% for each month prior to age 65. The maximum reduction is 25%. To qualify for benefits, the couple must have been married for 10 years or more; the divorced spouse must be unmarried; and the divorced spouse must not be entitled to a retirement or disability benefit based on a primary insurance amount which equals or exceeds one-half the worker's primary insurance amount.

More than one divorced spouse may be entitled on one worker's record. A divorced spouse's benefit will not reduce the benefits of the worker's other family members.

Dependent Children

When a worker is entitled to benefits, his or her unmarried dependent children are entitled to benefits equal to one-half of the worker's primary insurance amount. The child must either be under 18 years of age or be 18 or 19 years of age and a student attending primary or secondary school.

Dependent Grandchildren

A dependent grandchild, under the same conditions required of dependent children, is entitled to benefits equal to one-half the worker's primary insurance amount. An additional requirement is that the grandchild's parents must be dead or disabled.

Family Maximum

Family benefits based on a worker's account are limited to an maximum amount based on the worker's primary insurance amount. (See Soc. Sec. Act Sec. 203.) This amount is indexed. (See Soc. Sec. Act Sec. 215; 62 *Federal Register* 58762.) The maximum for 1999 is the sum of the following percentages:

- 150% of the first $645

- 272% of the primary insurance amount over $645 through $931

- 134% of the primary insurance amount over $931 through $1,214

- 175% of the primary insurance amount over $1,214

EXAMPLE

For a primary insurance amount of $1,250 in 1999, the family maximum would be $2,188.

150% of $645	$ 968
272% of ($931 − $645)	778
134% of ($1,214 − $931)	379
175% of ($1,250 − $1,214)	63
Family maximum	$ 2,188

Divorced spouse benefits are not included in the amounts deemed received by the family for purposes of the limitation.

Survivor Benefits

Surviving Spouse

A surviving spouse 65 years of age or older is generally entitled to benefits equal to 100% of the worker's primary insurance amount. (See Soc. Sec. Act Sec. 202.) If the worker was receiving a reduced benefit at death and the surviving spouse is age 65 or older, the surviving spouse's benefit will not exceed the greater of the amount the worker would be receiving if living, or 82.5% of the worker's primary insurance amount. Prior receipt of a reduced spouse's benefit will not cause a reduction of surviving spouse's benefits.

The benefits are reduced if the surviving spouse is age 60 to 64. The benefits are reduced $^{19}/_{40}$ of 1% for each month that benefits begin prior to the age of 65. The maximum reduction is 28.5%. The benefit is 75% of the deceased worker's primary insurance amount for a younger surviving spouse caring for a child eligible for benefits and under age 16.

In order to retain entitlement to the benefits, the surviving spouse must remain unmarried until attaining the age of 60. A disabled surviving spouse can begin receiving benefits at age 50.

Surviving Divorced Spouse

A surviving divorced spouse is generally entitled to the same benefits as that of a widow or widower. (See Soc. Sec. Act Sec. 202.) The surviving divorced spouse must have been married to the worker for at least 10 years and must not remarry before age 60.

Surviving Dependent Child

If a worker was fully insured or currently insured at death, a surviving dependent child may be entitled to a benefit equal to 75% of the worker's primary insurance amount. (See Soc. Sec. Act

Sec. 202.) The child must either be under 18 years of age or be 18 or 19 years of age and a student attending primary or secondary school. The child must be unmarried and must apply for benefits.

Surviving Dependent Grandchildren

A surviving dependent grandchild, under the same conditions required of surviving dependent children, is entitled to benefits equal to 75% of the worker's primary insurance amount. (See Soc. Sec. Act Sec. 202.) An additional requirement is that the grandchild's parents must be dead or disabled.

Surviving Dependent Parents

If a worker was providing over half of the support of a parent, the surviving parent can receive a benefit equal to 82.5% of the worker's primary insurance amount. (See Soc. Sec. Act Sec. 202.) The parent cannot be married. Both parents' benefits together cannot exceed 150% of the worker's primary insurance amount.

Family Maximum

The family maximum applies to the surviving family of a worker.

Recomputation of Benefits

As previously noted, some individuals receiving benefits continue to earn taxable wages and/or self-employment income, causing their benefits to be reduced if these earnings are too high. This causes a recomputation of benefits in two ways.

Individuals electing to receive benefits before full retirement age receive reduced monthly benefits. If, for any month when the individual was receiving benefits, these benefits were reduced due to excess earnings or the individual became entitled to a disability insurance benefit, the permanent reduction in benefits will be recomputed when the individual attains full retirement age. The early retirement period is reduced by these months and a new reduction percentage is computed treating only the remaining months as the early retirement period. (See Soc. Sec. Act Sec. 202.)

The primary insurance amount may also be recomputed if the worker's earnings are higher than some of the years included in the original computation. The recomputation is made as though the year, with respect to which it is made, is the last of the worker's computation base years. This annual recomputation never decreases the primary insurance amount.

Simultaneous Benefits

When both spouses have worked, each can receive benefits on their own record or on the record of their spouse. A similar situation occurs when children are eligible for benefits on both parents' records. Individuals eligible for benefits on more than one work record generally receive the larger amount.

If one of the spouses takes early retirement, that spouse takes a reduced benefit based on his or her own record. This reduction is permanent, even if he or she later elects to take a greater spouse's benefit. When the other spouse retires, the earlier-retiring spouse can then take the greater of his or her own reduced benefit or a reduced benefit based upon half of the later-retiring spouse's primary insurance benefit.

A widow(er)'s benefit will be permanently reduced if the deceased spouse was receiving a reduced benefit due to early retirement. However, surviving spouses do not have to suffer a permanent reduction in benefits upon his or her own early retirement after their spouse dies. A widow(er) can take reduced retirement benefits at age 62 and receive the full widow(er)'s benefit at age 65, or the individual can receive the widow(er)'s benefit at age 62 and still receive a full benefit based upon his or her own record at age 65. (A permanent reduction applies for workers born before 1928.) (See *Soc. Sec. Handbook,* SSA Pub. No. 65-008, 1997, Sec. 723.)

Lump-Sum Death Benefit

A one-time death benefit of $255 is payable to certain family members of a deceased worker. The benefit is payable to:

- The widow or widower of an insured worker if they were residing together at the time of death; or if not present.

- An individual eligible for surviving spouse or surviving dependent parent benefits; or if not present.

- Surviving children eligible for benefits. (See Soc. Sec. Act Sec. 202.)

Filing for Benefits

Workers nearing retirement age should contact their local Social Security Administration office. Employees of that office will be able to assist the worker in evaluating options for retirement and in filing the proper application.

Workers should file the application for benefits two or three months before they want to begin receiving benefits. A claim for the lump-sum death benefit must be filed within two years after the worker's death. (See Soc. Sec. Act Sec. 202.)

When a Worker Should Apply for Benefits

As previously discussed, a worker can begin receiving benefits as early as age 62, but with a permanent reduction in benefits. Although many factors must obviously be considered in making the retirement decision, an evaluation of the total dollars to be received from Social Security benefits could be helpful. The age at which an individual would break even would be computed as follows:

$$\frac{36 \text{ months of reduced benefit before age 65}}{\text{Permanent monthly reduction in benefit}} = \frac{\text{number of months}}{\text{past age 65}}$$

Note that this formula does not take into account the time value of money. Application of present-value assumptions would defer the break-even point to a later date.

EXAMPLE

Assume Mr. Jones's primary insurance amount was $1,251. His reduced benefit at age 62 would be $1,001. If Mr. Jones puts off retirement until age 65, how many years will it take for him to recoup the foregone income from age 62 to age 65 in the form of increased benefits beginning at age 65?

$$\frac{36 \text{ months} \times \$1,001}{\$1,251 - \$1,001} = \frac{\$36,036}{\$250} = 144 \text{ months or 12 years}$$

Consequently, Mr. Jones can retire at age 62 and be ahead, in terms of total dollars received, until age 77. Present-value computations would push the break-even date to a later age. It should be noted that at age 62 Mr. Jones's life expectancy is 16.9 years. (See Reg. Sec. 1.72-9.) (The life expectancy for a 62-year-old female is 20.3 years.)

The same logic can be applied to a spouse entitled to a worker's benefit but who will be entitled to a larger spouse's benefit when the other spouse later starts receiving benefits.

EXAMPLE

Both Mr. and Mrs. Smith are entitled to workers' benefits. Both are age 62. Mrs. Smith has retired, but Mr. Smith will work until he is 65. Mrs. Smith's primary insurance amount is $400, and her reduced benefit at age 62 is $320. When Mr. Smith retires at age 65, his primary insurance benefit will be $1,250. Mrs. Smith will be 65 at that time, and had she delayed retirement until she was 65, she would be entitled to a spouse's insurance benefit of $625, which would consist of her primary insurance benefit of $400 plus $225 additional spouse's benefit. However, since Mrs. Smith elected reduced benefits at age 62, her total benefit at age 65 will be $545 (her reduced benefit of $320 plus her spouse's benefit of $225). How many years would it take for her to recoup the lost income, had she waited until age 65 to receive her benefits?

$$\frac{36 \text{ months} \times \$320}{\$625 - \$545} = \frac{\$11,520}{\$80} = 144 \text{ months or 12 years}$$

Once again the time value of money would push the break-even point to a later date. Another consideration in this case might be that while Mr. Smith is still working the couple's income may be higher, resulting in a larger portion of Mrs. Smith's benefits being subject to income tax than would have been the case had she waited until Mr. Smith retired to start receiving benefits.

Taxation of Social Security Benefits

Computation of Taxable Amount

For years beginning after 1993, a portion of Social Security benefits are potentially taxable, based upon a two-tiered system. The system is based upon *modified adjusted gross income.* (See Sec. 86.)

Modified adjusted gross income is defined as the sum of the following:

- Adjusted gross income

- Tax-exempt interest

- The foreign-earned income exclusion, the U.S. possessions source income exclusion, and the Puerto Rico resident's income exclusion

When modified adjusted gross income plus one-half of Social Security benefits exceeds a base amount, Social Security benefits are included in gross income to the extent of the lesser of the following:

- One-half of Social Security benefits

- One-half of the amount by which the sum of modified adjusted gross income plus one-half of social security benefits exceeds the base amount

A second tier of taxation occurs when the sum of modified adjusted gross income and one-half of Social Security benefits exceeds a higher base amount. The amounts of the original base amount and the second-tier base amount are detailed in Table 3.4.

TABLE 3.4 Base Amounts

Filing Status	First-tier base amount	Second-tier base amount
Single or head of household	$25,000	$34,000
Married filing jointly	$32,000	$44,000
Married filing separately— unless living together	$25,000	$34,000
Married filing separately— living together	-0-	-0-

TABLE 3.4A Taxable Social Security

Step 1
Lesser of:

- 50% of Social Security benefits

- 50% of (modified adjusted gross income + 50% of Social Security benefits − first-tier base amount)

Step 2
Lesser of:

- Step 1 amount, not to exceed $6,000 ($4,500 for unmarried individuals) + 85% of (modified adjusted gross income + 50% of Social Security benefits − second-tier base amount)

- 85% of Social Security benefits

EXAMPLES

Mr. Smith is 67 years old. He has income from his retirement plan of $15,000 and Social Security benefits of $10,000. As a single individual, he would have an adjusted gross income of 15,000, computed as follows.

Retirement income	$15,000
Social Security included in gross income	0
Adjusted gross income	$15,000

Social Security included in gross income:

Lesser of the following:

- One-half of $10,000 = $5,000

- One-half of [$15,000 + 0.5($10,000) − $25,000] = 0

Mr. and Mrs. Jones are each 67 years old. Combined, they have income from their retirement plans of $30,000 and Social Security benefits of $20,000. As a married couple, their adjusted gross income would be $34,000, computed as follows.

Retirement income	$30,000
Social Security included in gross income	$4,000
Adjusted gross income	$34,000

Social Security included in gross income:

Lesser of the following:

- One-half of $20,000 = $10,000

- One-half of [$30,000 + 0.5($20,000) − $32,000] = $4,000

Mr. and Mrs. Jackson are very similar to Mr. and Mrs. Jones. They are each 67 years old. Together, they have income from their retirement plans of $30,000 and Social Security benefits of $20,000. However, they also have $10,000 of tax-exempt interest income. As a married couple, their adjusted gross income would be $39,000, computed as follows.

(continues)

Retirement income	$30,000
Social Security included in gross income	$9,000
Adjusted gross income	$39,000

Social security included in gross income:

Lesser of the following:

- One half of $20,000 = $10,000

- One half of [$30,000 + $10,000 + 0.5($20,000) − $32,000] = $9,000

Mr. and Mrs. Green have $100,000 of income from their retirement funds and $20,000 of Social Security benefits. As a married couple filing jointly, their adjusted gross income would be $117,000, computed as follows.

Retirement income	$100,000
Social Security included in gross income	$17,000
Adjusted gross income	$117,000

Social Security included in gross income:

Step 1
Lesser of the following:

- One half of $20,000 = $10,000

- One half of ($100,000 + 0.5($20,000) − $32,000) = $39,000

Step 2
Lesser of the following:

- Step 1 amount, not to exceed $6,000 + 0.85[$100,000 + 0.5($20,000) − $44,000] = $6,000 + $56,100 = $62,100

- 0.85 × $20,000 = $17,000

COMPUTATION AID: For a worksheet to compute Social Security benefits included in gross income, see Worksheet 3.2 on page 93.

Medicare and Medicaid

Medicare is a hospital and medical insurance program administered by the Social Security Administration. It is funded by premiums, payroll and self-employment taxes, and general federal taxes. Medicaid is a need-based hospital and medical program administered by state governments with oversight by the federal Health Care Financing Administration of the Department of Health and Human Services. It is financed by federal, state, and local taxes.

Medicare

Medicare has two parts. Part A consists of hospital benefits. Part B consists of supplementary medical insurance benefits.

Part A—Hospital Benefits for the Aged and Disabled

Individuals eligible for Medicare coverage without additional premium payments include:

- Individuals age 65 and older entitled to receive Social Security or railroad retirement benefits, even if not currently receiving benefits

- Individuals under age 65 who have received Social Security or railroad retirement disability benefits for 24 months

- Individuals with permanent kidney failure

Enrollment is automatic for individuals receiving Social Security or Railroad Retirement benefits. Other individuals, eligible for Social Security but not receiving benefits, must apply. For individuals with 30 to 40 quarters of covered employment, the monthly premium is $170. For individuals with less than 30 quarters of covered employment, the monthly premium in 1999 is $309.

Part A pays a portion of inpatient hospital and skilled-nursing-facility care, hospice care, and home health care.

For hospitalization in 1999, the individual pays a deductible of $768 for the first 60 days in the hospital. For the next 30 days, the individual pays $192 per day. After 90 days, the individual either pays all of the costs or may use up a one-time reserve of 60 days, paying a deductible of $384 per day.

For skilled-nursing-facility care in 1999, Medicare pays for the first 20 days of care. For the next 80 days, the individual pays $96.00 per day. After 100 days, the individual is responsible for all of the cost.

For home health care, Medicare pays the full approved cost.

Hospice care, for terminally ill individuals with a life expectancy of no more than six months, is paid in full by Medicare for 210 days.

The deductibles apply with respect to each benefit period. A benefit period begins the day a person enters the hospital and ends 60 days after the person leaves the hospital.

Part A generally covers the following:

- Semiprivate room, bed, and board
- Physician and nursing services while in the hospital
- Drugs administered while in the hospital
- Medical supplies
- Inpatient rehabilitation services
- Home health aid services
- Pain relief and symptom management services for the terminally ill

Part B—Supplementary Medical Benefits for the Aged and Disabled

Part B covers a portion of physicians' services and other outpatient medical expenses. It is optional and requires payment of a monthly premium. The premium was $45.50 in 1999. If Part B is not elected at the time Part A coverage begins, there will be a penalty in the form of larger premiums when it is elected later. After an annual deductible of $100, Medicare pays 80% of the covered costs.

Part B generally covers the following:

- Medical and surgical treatments

- Medical services and supplies such as ambulance transportation, artificial limbs, eyeglasses and lenses, and home dialysis equipment and support services

- Rental or purchase of medical equipment used in the home

- Mammography cancer screening

- Physical, speech, and occupational therapy

- Outpatient services such as emergency room care, lab tests, X rays, and radiology services

- Home health aide services

Medicaid

Medicaid is for categorically needy or medically needy individuals. Many individuals' need for Medicaid occurs after a lengthy illness when Medicare's nursing care coverage has been exhausted. The cost of the long-term illness may then use up the individual's savings and other assets, leaving the individual needy and qualifying for Medicaid.

The 1988 Medicare Catastrophic Coverage Act contained provisions to allow a spouse to keep some of his or her assets and income without affecting the qualification of the ailing spouse for Medicaid. (See Soc. Sec. Act Sec. 1924.) In addition, assets may be transferred to other individuals without penalty if the transfer is completed early enough. However, if the transfer is completed within 36 months before the date the ailing spouse is institutionalized or, if later the date application is made for Medicaid, a penalty will be imposed in the form of reduced benefits. (See Soc. Sec. Act Sec. 1917(c).)

Medicaid is jointly administered by the states and the federal government. A comprehensive discussion of the program is difficult, since each state has some discretion as to eligibility and services. In addition, the current political environment is likely to result in new legislation and/or administrative pronouncements from time to time. Local legal counsel should be consulted when planning for the financial implications of a long-term illness.

Additional Information

A wealth of information is available from the Social Security Administration. In addition to many brochures and other helpful information available at local Social Security offices, the *Social Security Handbook* (SSA Pub. No. 65-008, 1997) can be purchased from the U.S. Government Printing Office. Information is also available on the Social Security Administration's web site—http://www.ssa.gov. Information on Medicare and Medicaid is available on the Health Care Financing Administration's web site—http://www.hcfa.gov.

Worksheet 3.1   Computation Aid Social Security 1

Computation of Primary Insurance Amount—1999

Year	Age	Actual earnings	Maximum income	Lesser of actual or maximum	Average of total wages	Indexed earnings note 1	Not included note 2	Benefit computation years
1954			3,600		3,155.64			
1955			4,200		3,301.44			
1956			4,200		3,532.36			
1957			4,200		3,641.72			
1958			4,200		3,673.80			
1959			4,800		3,855.88			
1960			4,800		4,007.12			
1961			4,800		4,086.76			
1962			4,800		4,291.40			
1963			4,800		4,396.64			
1964			4,800		4,576.32			
1965			4,800		4,658.72			
1966			6,600		4,938.36			
1967			6,600		5,213.44			
1968			7,800		5,571.76			
1969			7,800		5,893.76			
1970			7,800		6,186.24			
1971			7,800		6,497.08			
1972			9,000		7,133.80			
1973			10,800		7,580.16			
1974			13,200		8,030.76			
1975			14,100		8,630.92			
1976			15,300		9,226.48			
1977			16,500		9,779.44			
1978			17,700		10,556.03			
1979			22,900		11,479.46			
1980			25,900		12,513.46			
1981			29,700		13,773.10			
1982			32,400		14,531.34			

(continues)

Worksheet 3.1   Computation Aid Social Security 1 (*continued*)

Computation of Primary Insurance Amount—1999

Year	Age	Actual earnings	Maximum income	Lesser of actual or maximum	Average of total wages	Indexed earnings note 1	Not included note 2	Benefit computation years
1983			35,700		15,239.24			
1984			37,800		16,135.07			
1985			39,600		16,822.51			
1986			42,000		17,321.82			
1987			43,800		18,426.51			
1988			45,000		19,334.04			
1989			48,000		20,099.55			
1990			51,300		21,027.98			
1991			53,400		21,811.60			
1992			55,500		22,935.42			
1993			57,600		23,132.67			
1994			60,600		23,753.53			
1995			61,200		24,705.66			
1996			62,700		25,913.90			
1997			65,400		27,426.00			65,400
1998			68,400					68,400
1999			72,600					
Total								

Note 1

Indexed earnings = lesser of actual or maximum

$$\times \frac{\text{average of total wages—1997}}{\text{average of total wages—year being indexed}}$$

Note 2

Use only the benefit computation years—the number of elapsed years minus 5. Elapsed years are the number of calendar years after the year of attainment of age 21 and prior to

Worksheet 3.1　Computation Aid Social Security 1 (*continued*)

Computation of Primary Insurance Amount—1999

age 62—generally 40 years. Consequently, benefit computation years are generally 35 years. Exclude the other years with the smallest indexed earnings.

$$\text{Average indexed monthly earnings (AIME)} = \frac{\text{total of benefit computation years}}{\text{number of months (generally } 35 \times 12)}$$

Primary Insurance Amount

90% of first $505 or less of AIME　　　　　　_____

32% of any AIME above $505 to $3,043　　　　_____

15% of any AIME above $3,043　　　　　　　_____

Primary Insurance Amount　　　　　　　　_____

Worksheet 3.2   Computation Aid Social Security 2

Social Security Benefits Included in Gross Income

Step 1:

Social Security benefits		_____
Multiply by		50%
50% of Social Security benefits		(A)_____
Adjusted gross income	_____	
Plus: tax-exempt interest	_____	
Plus: foreign earned income exclusion	_____	
Equals: modified adjusted gross income		_____
Plus: 50% of Social Security benefits		_____
Less: first-tier base amount ($32,000, $25,000 or $0)		_____
Total		_____
Multiply by		50%
		(B)_____
Lesser of (A) or (B)		_____

If modified adjusted gross income plus one-half of Social Security benefits does not exceed the second-tier base amounts, do not complete Step 2.

Worksheet 3.2   Computation Aid Social Security 2 (*continued*)

Step 2:

Social Security benefits		_____
Multiply by		× 85%
85% of Social Security benefits		(C)_____
Modified adjusted gross income (from Step 1)	_____	
Plus: 50% of Social Security benefits	_____	
Less: Second-tier base amount ($44,000, $34,000 or $0)	_____	
Total	_____	
Multiply by	× 85%	
	_____	
Plus: Step 1 amount, not to exceed $6,000 ($4,500 for unmarried individuals)	_____	
		(D)_____
Lesser of (C) or (D)		==========

Transfer of a Closely Held Business

A closely held business often represents a significant portion of the wealth of many individuals or couples. Transferring ownership of these businesses at the lowest possible tax cost may become a primary tax-planning objective of many such individuals. In some cases maintaining control over the business with the psychic and financial security that ownership and control offer may also be an important planning objective.

In this section several types of business organizations and the tax-planning opportunities offered by each are discussed.

Sole Proprietorships

Tax-planning opportunities are somewhat limited when disposing of a sole proprietorship. Corporations and limited partnerships offer substantially greater opportunities for tax planning than does the sole proprietorship. Therefore it may be desirable to convert to one of these forms as part of the overall tax-planning process. The use of these forms of organization will be discussed in a later section. In this section, the tax implications of the sale of a sole proprietorship and some of the tax-saving opportunities related to the passing of a sole proprietorship through an estate will be discussed. It will be assumed that in instances where the sole proprietor is a married individual, it is the estate of the second spouse to die that is being discussed. Estate tax can always be avoided in the estate of the first spouse through the use of the unlimited marital deduction. It is also assumed that any bypass trust established by the will of the first spouse has been funded with assets other than those from the sole proprietorship.

Sale of a Sole Proprietorship

The tax consequences of the sale of a sole proprietorship will vary, depending on the assets held in the business. The sale of accounts receivable and inventories will result in ordinary gain or loss. The sale of investments in stocks and bonds will yield short-term or long-term capital gain or loss, depending on whether the investments have been held for more than one year. The sale of depreciable personality generates ordinary income to the extent of recapture under Sec. 1245. Any remaining gain and losses will be treated under Sec. 1231. Gains on the sale of real estate will be ordinary to the extent of recapture under Sec. 1250, with remaining gains and losses subject to Sec. 1231. Disposition of intangible assets, including goodwill, generally result in capital gain or loss. However, intangibles acquired after August 10, 1993 (or after July 25, 1991, if so elected), that are subject to amortization under Sec. 197 will be treated as sales of depreciable personalty and will therefore be subject to the provisions of Sec. 1231. Sales of patents in the hands of a holder as defined by Code Sec. 1235 will always result in long-term capital gain or loss.

As indicated in the previous paragraph, gains or losses on the sale of certain properties are subject to the provisions of Sec. 1231. This section provides, with certain exceptions, that where gains and losses result in a net gain they are to be treated as long-term capital gains and losses. However, if the gains and losses result in a net loss, then all gains and losses are to be treated as ordinary gains and losses. Thus the taxpayer gets the best of both worlds, with ordinary losses generally being fully deductible and long-term capital gains generally being subject to a maximum tax rate of 20%.

The primary exception to Sec. 1231 is for unrecaptured 1231 losses that have occurred in the previous five tax years. To the extent of these unrecaptured losses, net 1231 gains will be treated as ordinary income.

EXAMPLE

Mr. Jones has net Sec. 1231 gains of $20,000 for Year 6. Mr. Jones has realized the following net Sec. 1231 gains and losses for the years Year 1 through Year 5:

Year	Gain (or loss)
1	$(15,000)
2	-0-
3	4,000
4	2,000
5	-0-

Mr. Jones's unrecaptured losses for the five-year look-back period are $9,000 ($15,000 − $4,000 − $2,000). Therefore the Year 6 gain will be treated as $9,000 of ordinary income and $11,000 long-term capital gain.

The previous example would indicate that a taxpayer contemplating the sale of a business should consider segregating Sec. 1231 gains and losses into different years where possible. If the taxpayer has no unrecaptured losses for prior years, assets that would result in gains should be sold first and would generally be taxed as long-term capital, with a resulting maximum tax rate of 20%. Section 1231 gains that escaped recapture under Sec. 1250, to the extent of depreciation, would be taxed at a maximum rate of 25%.

Assets that would result in losses could then be sold in a later year and treated as ordinary losses. Unfortunately, the inverse cannot (and should not) be done. If the losses are realized first, the gains in later years will be ordinary to the extent of the losses.

Prior to the enactment of Sec. 197 providing for the amortization of intangibles, it was often difficult for buyers and sellers to agree on the allocation of the purchase price when a business was sold for a lump sum. The seller generally wished to allocate the smallest possible amount to accounts receivable, inventory, depreciable personalty, and other assets that would yield ordinary gain on the sale. The seller much preferred to allocate as much as possible to the sale of land, buildings, goodwill, and other assets whose sale would generate long-term capital gain. This was particularly true if goodwill was involved, since goodwill would generate long-term capital gain. The buyer, on the other hand, wished to allocate as much as possible to accounts receivable and inventories, whose cost would be deductible in a very short time frame. From the buyer's viewpoint the next most desirable allocation was to depreciable property, including buildings, whose cost could be recovered through cost-recovery allowances. From the buyer's viewpoint, the least desirable allocation would be to goodwill, which could not be amortized and generated no tax benefit until some subsequent sale of the business sometime in the future.

With the advent of Sec. 197, the viewpoint of the buyer will be substantially different. Accounts receivable, inventory, and depreciable assets have a short recovery period and are still attractive targets for allocation. Buildings, which now have a 39-year recovery period (27.5 years for residential property), are now much less attractive targets than goodwill, which can be amortized over a 15-year period under Sec. 197. While allocation of the purchase price in the lump-sum sale of a business should always be based on appraisals and other objective evidence, some leeway is always available as allocation decisions are made. Section 197 should facilitate agreement between buyers and sellers in this area.

When a business is sold, tax savings can usually be realized through the use of the installment method under Sec. 453. If payments are to be received in any year after the year of sale, gain can be reported in proportion to cash received each year. Use of the installment method is mandatory unless the seller elects out of its use.

EXAMPLE

Mrs. Smith sells her rental property for $1,000,000. She is to receive 10 equal installments of $70,000 (plus interest at the current market rate) beginning in the year of sale. The purchaser also assumes a mortgage of $300,000 on the property. Mrs. Smith's basis in the property is $400,000. Straight-line depreciation has been used on the property.

Mrs. Smith has a gain of $600,000, which can be reported $60,000 each year, computed as follows:

$$\frac{\text{Gain}}{\text{Contract price (sales price} - \text{mortgage)}}$$

$$\times \text{ annual payment} = \text{amount reported}$$

$$\frac{\$600,000}{(\$1,000,000 - \$300,000)} \times \$70,000 = \$60,000$$

Interest received will be accounted for separately and reported each year as received.

The installment method cannot be used to report gain on the sale of property held for resale in the ordinary course of business (inventory), gain on sale of publicly traded securities, or gain on sale of depreciable property to controlled corporations or partnerships. (See Secs. 453(b)(2) and 453(g).) Where depreciable property is sold at a gain that is subject to recapture under Secs. 1245 and 1250, the gain that is ordinary under these sections must all be recognized in the year of sale. (See Sec. 453(i).)

EXAMPLE

Assume that in the previous example an accelerated method of depreciation had been used on the rental property, resulting in recapture of $100,000 under Sec. 1250. Mrs. Smith's recognized gain in the year of sale is $150,000, computed as follows:

Sec. 1250 gain — ordinary income	$100,000
Installment gain — 1231 gain:	
$\dfrac{\$500,000}{\$700,000} \times \$70,000$	$50,000
	$150,000

The taxpayer would report $50,000 each year for the next nine years, computed in the normal manner.

Sections 453(e)(1) and (2) place restrictions on the use of the installment where the purchaser and seller are related parties. If the purchaser disposes of the property that was the subject of the installment sale within two years of the sale, the purchaser will be treated as having received all remaining payments due under the contract in the year of this second disposition, and all unrecognized gain will be recognized immediately. Related parties are those described in Sec. 318(a) or Sec. 267(b).

Installment sales to such related parties do offer some tax-deferral possibilities to family units, as long they are patient and can wait out the two-year period before making a final disposition of the property.

EXAMPLE

A father sells real property with a basis of $100,000 to his son. The property has a fair market value of $200,000, and the son agrees to pay his father $20,000 per year for 10 years. The father does not elect out of the installment method and therefore recognizes $10,000 of the gain each year. After two years the son sells the property to an unrelated third party for $210,000. Since the son's basis is $200,000, he reports only a $10,000 gain on the sale. The family now has the full proceeds from the sale but may still defer a substantial part of the gain to future periods, since such gain will be recognized only as the son makes annual payments to his father.

Private Annuities

Private annuities offer some excellent opportunities for the transfer of a closely held business to the next generation. A private annuity is any annuity arrangement issued by anyone not regularly engaged in the business of issuing annuity contracts. The taxation of private annuities is very similar to that of commercial annuities issued by insurance companies and other financial institutions and is covered in the "Taxation of Periodic Payments—Annuities" section in Chapter 2 of this book. Private annuities differ from commercial annuities in that they are almost always issued in exchange for property other than cash, whereas commercial annuities are usually issued for cash. The typical private arrangement has the property owner transferring property to another individual, usually a younger family member, in exchange for a promise to pay the transferor a monthly or annual payment for the transferor's life. If the transferors are a married couple, the annuity could be made payable over the joint lives of the spouses.

The primary tax advantage of the private annuity is that it removes any future appreciation on the property transferred from the estate of the transferor and places it in the hands of the next generation. However, while the property is removed from the estate of the transferor, payments made by the transferee are placed back in the estate of the transferor. In the case of a single transferor the annuity does not result in any additional amount being included in the estate of the transferor since payments cease at his or her death. However, in the case of an annuity payable over more than one life the value of the annuity to the surviving annuitant, usually a spouse, will be included in the estate of the first to die if the decedent was the owner of the property transferred. (See Sec. 2039.)

Gift tax is incurred on the exchange of property for a private annuity only where the present value of the annuity is less than value of the property transferred. Private annuities are valued under the rules found at Reg. Sec. 20.2031-7. This regulation contains tables with valuation factors for interest rates from 4.2% to 14%. The rate used will be equal to 120% of the federal midterm rate for the month of the transaction, rounded to the nearest 0.2 of one percent.

EXAMPLE

Mr. Davis, who has a 24-year life expectancy, transfers a capital asset to Mr. Davison in exchange for a promise to pay Mr. Davis $20,000 per year for life. The adjusted basis of the property to Mr. Davis is $100,000, and an appraisal indicates that its current value is $200,000. The valuation tables for Davis's age and the current federal rate indicate a present value of the annuity to be $167,300.

Tax results to Mr. Davis are:

- Mr. Davis has made a gift of $32,700 ($200,000 − $167,300) to Mr. Davison.

- Mr. Davis has a capital gain of $67,300 ($167,300 − $100,000), which will be recognized at a rate of $2,804 ($67,300/24) each year.

- Mr. Davis will have a tax-free return of capital of $4,167 ($100,000/24) each year.

- Mr. Davis will have ordinary income of $13,029 ($20,000 − $2,084 − $4,167) each year, which is the interest element of the annuity. (See Rev. Rul. 69-74, 1969-1 C.B. 43.)

In accordance with the general rules of Sec. 72 for annuities, if Mr. Davis lives beyond his life expectancy the entire payment will be recognized each year as income. If he fails to live for 24 years any unrecovered basis will be deductible on his final return.

The most important disadvantage of a private annuity is the tax treatment required for the taxpayer making the annuity payments. No interest deduction is allowed for any portion of the payments made by the payor. All payments made are added to the basis of the property acquired. If the property is held until the death of the transferor, the basis of the property for depreciation, gain, and loss will be the total of all payments made, adjusted for depreciation allowed. The initial basis for depreciation will be the present value of the annuity payments to be made. If the property is disposed of before all annuity payments are made a dual basis is created. The basis for loss will be the sum of all payments made to the date of disposition, adjusted for depreciation taken. The basis for gain will be the sum of all payments made to date, increased by the present value of future payments to be made under the annuity contract, adjusted for depreciation taken. (See Rev. Rul. 55-119, 1955-1 C.B. 352.).

Inclusion of a Sole Proprietorship in an Estate

As indicated in the introduction to this section, estate tax savings can usually be realized by changing the organizational structure of the business to a corporation or a limited partnership. If, however, the decision is made to pass the sole proprietorship through an estate, there are several provisions which will either reduce the tax or lessen the burden of payment of those taxes. This section will examine Sec. 2032A, Special Use Valuation; Sec. 2057, Family-Owned Business Interests; Sec. 6161, Discretionary Extension of Time to Pay Estate Taxes; and Sec. 6166, Extension of Time When the Estate Consists Largely of an Interest in a Closely Held Business.

Inclusion of a Sole Proprietorship in an Estate—Special Use Valuation—Sec. 2032A

The provisions of Sec. 2032A allow real estate used in a farming business or other trade or business to be valued for estate tax purposes at its use value rather than its highest or best-use value. This provision is intended to provide relief to closely held businesses where inclusion in the estate at full value would create liquidity problems for the estate and might result in a forced sale of some or all of the assets of the business to pay estate taxes.

The maximum reduction in value in the gross estate as a result of this section cannot exceed $750,000. (See Sec. 2032A(a)(2).)

EXAMPLES

Mr. Simms owns real estate currently used as a vegetable farm, with a use value of $400,000. The property is located near a large city and has a development value of $800,000. If Sec. 2032A is elected, the real estate will be included in the gross estate at a value of $400,000.

Assume the same facts as in the previous example, except the development value of the real estate is $1,200,000. The real estate would be included in the gross estate at a value of $450,000 ($1,200,000 − $750,000).

Section 2032A(e)(7) provides guidance in determining use value for farms. This section provides that farms shall be valued by the following procedure:

- Taking the average cash rental for comparable land for the five most recent years

- Subtracting the average of state and local real estate taxes for the same period

- Dividing the result by the average annual effective interest rate for all new Federal Land Loans for this period

If there are no comparable cash rentals, then average annual net share rentals may be used. If neither cash or net share rentals are available, then farmland may be valued by the methods established for other closely held businesses.

COMPUTATION AID: For a worksheet to compute the alternate valuation of a farm, see Worksheet 4.3 on page 140.

Section 2032A(e)(8) provides guidance for cases where Sec. 2032A(e)(7) does not apply. This section provides that the use value for real estate used in farming or other closely held businesses shall be valued by using some or all of the following factors:

- Capitalization of income

- Capitalization of fair rental values

- Assessed values

- Comparable sales of real estate far enough removed from a metropolitan or resort area so that nonagricultural use is not a significant factor

- Any other factor that is a fair indicator of the use value of the real estate

Section 2032A is an elective provision, with the election made by the executor or administrator of the estate. The election must be made on the estate tax return and is irrevocable. The election must be accompanied by an agreement to the election signed by all parties having an interest in the property and consenting to the application of Sec. 2032A(c) relating to recapture of estate tax discussed in the text that follows.

Section 2032A imposes a number of requirements that must be met to be eligible for the election. The real property being so valued must be *qualified real property*. Qualified real property is "property located in the United States which was acquired from or passed from the decedent to a qualified heir of the decedent and which, on the date of the decedent's death, was being used for a qualified use by the decedent or a member of the decedent's family. . . ." Further, to be qualified real property, 50% or more of the adjusted value of the gross estate must consist of real and personal property used in the farming business or other trade or business, and 25% or more of the adjusted value of the gross estate must be real property so used. (See Sec. 2032A(b)(1)(A).)

For purposes of the 25% and 50% tests, adjusted value of the gross estate means the gross estate reduced by amounts allowable as a deduction by paragraph (4) of Sec. 2053(a) for mortgages and other indebtedness on property included in the gross estate. For purposes of these tests the adjusted value of the gross estate is computed using the highest and best use of the property, rather than its use value. (See Sec. 2032A(a)(3).)

COMPUTATION AID: For a worksheet to determine if these tests are met, see Worksheet 4.1 on page 137.

EXAMPLE

Mrs. Johnson dies, leaving real estate with a use value of $300,000 and a highest and best value of $900,000, and personal property with a value of $500,000, all used in a trade or business. The decedent left other property with a value of $1,300,000. The decedent had no indebtedness. The adjusted value of the gross estate is $2,700,000 ($900,000 + $500,000 + $1,300,000). Since $900,000 is more than 25% of $2,700,000, and $1,400,000 is more than 50% of $2,700,000, the estate meets both tests and, if other requirements are met, is eligible to make the election.

To qualify for election, the following requirements also apply:

- The decedent was a resident or citizen of the United States at the time of his death.

- During the eight-year period ending on the date of the decedent's death, there were periods aggregating five years or more during which the property was owned by the decedent or a member of his family and was used by the decedent or family member for a qualifying use (i.e., as a farm or other trade or business).

- There was material participation by the decedent or family in the farm or other business

- The property was designated in the agreement referred to above.

For retired decedents the eight-year period ends on the date the decedent began receiving Social Security payments and received such payments continuously until his death. For disabled decedents the eight-year period ends on the date the decedent became disabled and remained disabled continuously until his death. (See Sec. 2032A(b)(4).)

Members of the family include:

- The individual's spouse

- The individual's ancestors

- Lineal descendants of the individual, of the individual's spouse, or of the individual's parents

- The spouses of any such lineal descendants

A legally adopted child of an individual is treated as a child of the individual. (See Sec. 2032A(e)(2).)

Material participation for this provision should not be confused with material participation as defined by Sec. 469 relating to passive losses. Section 2032A(e)(6) provides that material participation should be determined in a manner similar to that used for Sec. 1402(a) relating to net earnings from self-employment. Regulation Sec. 20.2032A-3(e)(2) states that "[no] single factor is determinative of the presence of material participation, but physical work and participation in management decisions are the principal factors to be considered. As a minimum, the decedent and/or a family member must regularly advise or consult with the other managing party on the operation of the business."

COMPUTATION AID: For a checklist of attachment to an election to use an alternate valuation, see Worksheet 4.2 on page 138.

Once the election is made and the estate tax reduction realized, the qualifying real estate must continue to be used for the qualifying purpose by a qualified heir for at least 10 years, or a recapture tax is imposed. There is no phaseout of the recapture tax. Thus, a cessation of qualified use 9 years and 11 months after the decedent's death results in full recapture. A qualified heir is a member of the decedent's family, as previously described, who acquired the property from the decedent or to whom such property passed from the decedent. If a qualified heir passes an interest in the property to a member of his family and that family member continues the qualified use, that person becomes a qualified heir, and recapture is not imposed. (See Sec. 2032A(c)(1) and Sec. 2032A(c)(1).)

The amount of the recapture tax is the lesser of the reduction in the estate tax as a result of election or the excess of the amount realized on disposition of the interest over the use value included in the estate with regard to the disposed interest. (See Sec. 2032A(c)(2)(A).) If a partial disposition is made the recapture applies only to the interest disposed of. The tax is imposed on the qualified heir who disposes of or discontinues the qualified use of the property. (See Sec. 2032A(c)(5).) The additional tax becomes due and payable six months after the date of the disposition or cessation of the qualified use. (See Sec. 2032A(c)(4).) Interest is assessed on the recapture tax beginning on the date it becomes due and payable. (See Rev. Rul. 81-308, 1981-2 C.B. 176.) There are special provisions for the disposition of timber (Sec. 2032A(c)(2)(E)), involuntary conversions (Sec. 2032A(h)), and like-kind exchanges (Sec. 2032A(i)). If the qualifying heir dies prior to the expiration of the 10-year period, the recapture period ceases. (See Sec. 2032A(c).)

Tax-planning opportunities are somewhat limited with regard to Sec. 2032A. The primary predeath opportunities are in the area of qualifying for the election under the 25% and 50% requirements. If the farm or trade or business property do not equal or exceed these percentages of an individual's assets, gifts of some of the nonfarm or nonbusiness assets or the acquisition of additional farm or business assets may raise these assets to qualifying levels.

EXAMPLE

Mr. Wright, a farmer, has the following assets:

Personalty used in the farm operation	$150,000
Real estate used in the farm operation	$200,000
Other assets	$400,000
Total assets	$750,000

Should Mr. Wright die, the estate would not be eligible to elect Sec. 2032A. The real estate comprises 27% of the total assets, but the realty and personalty make up only 47% of the total assets. If, however, Mr. Wright makes gifts of $50,000 or more out of nonfarm assets, the percentage requirements would be met.

Mr. Wright could also meet the percentage requirements by acquiring additional farm personalty with a cost of at least $25,000 in exchange for other nonfarm assets.

Advance planning is necessary to effect the desired results in the previous example. Section 2035(d)(3) requires that any gifts made by the decedent within three years of death must be included in the adjusted value of the gross estate for purposes of determining if the 25% and 50% tests are met.

The Internal Revenue Service has taken the position that Sec. 2032A cannot be elected where minority and/or marketability discounts have been used to determine the fair market value of the property. One circuit court has allowed the use of such discounts to determine the highest and best use value before applying the $750,000 limitation. (See *Hoover Estate v. Commissioner,* No. 94-9018 [10th Circuit, 11/1/95, reversing 102 TC 777 (1994)].)

Family-Owned Business Deduction

Sec. 2057 was added by the Taxpayer Relief Act of 1997, modified by the IRS Restructuring and Reform Act of 1998, and will be effective for the estates of decedents dying after December

31, 1997. Sec. 2057 allows for the deduction of the value of certain family-owned business interests from the gross estate. Generally, the deduction is the lesser of the following amounts:

- The adjusted value of the decedent's qualified family-owned business interests

- The excess of $1,300,000 over the applicable exclusion amount in effect with respect to the decedent's estate

The potential amount of the exclusion will decrease as the applicable exclusion increases, as shown in Table 4.1. As a result, only the value of qualified business interests in excess of $1,300,000 is subject to the estate tax.

Because the applicable exemption amount reduces taxes at the lower end of the tax rates, and the business deduction amount reduces taxes at the maximum rates, the tax savings provided by the deduction decrease as the applicable exemption amount increases over time. Consequently, the executor may elect to deduct up to $675,000 of qualified family-owned business interests. If the maximum $675,000 deduction is elected, the applicable exemption amount is limited to $625,000. If the deduction is less than $675,000, the exclusion amount is increased by the

TABLE **4.1 Business Deduction Exclusion**

Year	Applicable exemption amount	Business deduction amount
1997	$ 600,000	None
1998	625,000	$675,000
1999	650,000	650,000
2000 and 2001	675,000	625,000
2002 and 2003	700,000	600,000
2004	850,000	450,000
2005	950,000	350,000
2006 and after	1,000,000	300,000

excess of $675,000 over the amount of deduction allowed. The exclusion amount can never exceed the amount scheduled for that year. (See Sec. 2057(a).)

COMPUTATION AID: For a worksheet to determine the amount of the deduction and unified credit, see Worksheet 4.5 on page 142.

EXAMPLE

Ms. Wright dies in 2006. Her estate of $1,550,000 includes a qualified family-owned business interest of $800,000. If no election is made, the family-owned business deduction of $300,000 will reduce the taxable estate to $1,250,000. The estate tax will be $102,500—$448,300 less the applicable unified credit of $345,800. If the maximum deduction is elected, the family-owned business deduction will be $675,000, reducing the taxable estate to $875,000. The applicable exemption amount is $625,000 with an applicable unified credit of $202,050. The estate tax would then be $95,000—$297,050 less the unified credit of $202,050. The tax savings resulting from the election would be $7,500.

In order to claim the deduction, an ownership requirement must be met; the decedent must be a U.S. citizen or resident at the time of death; the executor must elect the special tax treatment; and a recapture agreement signed by each person having an interest in the property must be filed.

In order to be treated as a qualified family-owned business, an ownership test must be satisfied. A qualified family-owned business is a trade or business which meets one of the following conditions:

- At least 50% ownership by one family

- At least 70% ownership by two families

- At least 90% ownership by three families

If the trade or business is held by more than one family, the decedent's family must own at least 30% (See Sec. 2057(e)(1).)

Members of the family include:

- The individual's spouse

- The individual's ancestors

- Lineal descendants of the individual, of the individual's spouse, or of the individual's parents

- The spouses of any such lineal descendants.

A legally adopted child of an individual is treated as a child of the individual. (See Sec. 2057(i) referring to 2032A(e)(1).)

If the trade or business is held through a corporation, the ownership test requires that the required percentage ownership include both the total combined voting power of all classes of voting stock and the total value of all shares of all classes of stock. If the trade or business is held through a partnership, the correct percentage ownership applies to the capital interest in the partnership. The trade or business will not meet the ownership requirements if the business's, or a related entity's, stock or securities were publicly traded within the three years preceding the date of death. (See Sec. 2057(e).)

In order to qualify for the deduction, the aggregate value of the decedent's qualified family-owned businesses that are passed to qualified heirs must exceed 50% of the decedent's adjusted gross estate. Qualified heirs include any member of the decedent's family who acquired the property from the decedent. (See Sec. 2057(i) referring to Sec. 2032A(i).) The definition of qualified heirs also includes any active employee of the trade or business to which the qualified family-owned business interest relates if such employee has been employed by such trade or business for a period of at least 10 years before the date of the decedent's death. (See Sec. 2057(i).) The value of a qualified family-owned business does not include passive assets or excess cash held by the business.

The 50% test is applied to the following fraction. The numerator consists of:

- The adjusted value of the qualified family-owned business interests includible in the gross estate and passing to a qualified heir, *plus*

■ Gifts of such interests to members of the family (other than the spouse) that have been held continuously held by members of the family, *less*

■ Debts of the estate other than mortgages on the principal residence, educational or medical loans, and other indebtedness up to $10,000

The denominator is equal to:

■ The gross estate, *less*

■ Any indebtedness of the estate, *plus*

■ Lifetime transfers of qualified business interests made to members of the family and held continuously by the members, transfers to the decedent's spouse made within 10 years of the date of death, and any other transfers made by the decedent within three years of death (except nontaxable transfers to members of the family). (See Sec. 2057(c).)

COMPUTATION AID: For a worksheet to determine if the estate qualifies for this deduction, see Worksheet 4.4 on page 141.

The decedent or members of the family must have owned and materially participated in the trade or business for at least five of the last eight years preceding the date of death. A qualified heir must materially participate in the trade or business for at least five years of any eight-year period during the ten years following the date of death. (See Sec. 2057(b).) If this participation requirement is not met, the tax savings of excluding the family-owned business interest must be recaptured. If the heir ceases to participate within six years, 100% of that heir's share of the tax is due. The recapture schedule is provided in Table 4.2.

The percentage is applied to the additional estate tax that would have been due if the deduction had not been taken, less the actual amount of estate tax liability for the estate. (See Sec. 2057(f).)

The only planning to be done under this provision would be to position an individual's investments and business interests so

TABLE 4.2 Tax Recapture Schedule

Year participation ends	Percentage of tax recaptured
6	100
7	80
8	60
9	40
10	20

that the quantitative tests will be met. Gifts will not be effective, since most gifts are included in the 50% test.

EXAMPLE

Refer to the previous example. Again, Mr. Wright is a farmer. Upon his death, the farm will pass equally to Mrs. Wright and his son. Mr. Wright has the following assets:

Personalty used in the farm operation	$150,000
Real estate used in the farm operation	$200,000
Other assets	$400,000
Total assets	$750,000

The personalty and real estate used in the farm operation comprise a family-owned business.

Should Mr. Wright die, the estate would not be eligible to elect Sec. 2057. The family-owned business, the realty and personalty, make up only 47% of the total assets. Since gifts would continue to be included in the denominator and/or numerator, they would not affect qualification for the deduction.

Mr. Wright could meet the percentage requirements by acquiring additional farm personalty with a cost of at least $25,000 in exchange for other nonfarm assets. Care should be taken that any such assets acquired not be treated as passive assets.

Extensions of Time for Payment of Estate Tax

Estate taxes are due and payable on the estate tax return due date, which is nine months from the date of death of the decedent. This is true even when the due date for filing the return is extended. There are, however, two provisions for delaying the payment of estate taxes in certain circumstances.

Sec. 6161 provides authority for the Internal Revenue Service to extend the time for payment for any reasonable time (not to exceed 10 years) upon demonstration by the estate of reasonable cause for delay in payment. Reasonable cause is a less-demanding standard than undue hardship, and an extension may be granted where the executor experiences difficulty in marshaling the assets or where a significant portion of the liquid assets of the estate will be realized in future periods. Use of this provision is at the discretion of the Internal Revenue Service, and there are no quantitative standards for its use.

Sec. 6166 provides a method for payment of estate taxes on an installment basis where more than 35% of the adjusted gross estate consists of an interest in a farm or other closely held business. The adjusted gross estate is the gross estate less the deductions allowed by Sec. 2053 for expenses, indebtedness, and taxes and by Sec. 2054 for casualty and theft losses during administration.

COMPUTATION AID: For a worksheet to determine if the estate would qualify of this method of payment, see Worksheet 4.6 on page 143.

An interest in a closely held business includes the following:

- A sole proprietorship

- A partnership if 20% or more of the capital interest of the partnership is included in the gross estate or the partnership has 15 or fewer partners

- The stock in a corporation if 20% or more of the value of the voting stock is included in the gross estate or the corporation has 15 or fewer stockholders.

For purposes of the 20% and 15-partner or -stockholder rules, a partnership interest or stock owned by the decedent and a surviving spouse as community property, as tenants in common, or as joint tenants is considered as owned by the decedent. Partnership interests and stock owned by family members as defined by Sec. 267 are considered as if they were owned by the decedent. (See Sec. 6166.)

Interests in two or more qualifying business interests can be aggregated for purposes of meeting the 35% rule if 20% or more of the value of each such business is included in the decedent's adjusted gross estate. For purposes of this requirement, interests held by the surviving spouse as community property, tenants in common, or joint tenancy with the decedent are treated as though owned by the decedent. (See Sec. 6166(c).)

If the just-stated conditions are met, the executor may elect to defer the payment of estate tax for a period of up to five years and may thereafter pay the tax in two or more (but not more than ten) annual installments. (See Sec. 6166(a).) Interest on the deferred tax must be paid annually until the first installment is due. Interest thereafter would be paid with each installment. Interest on the first $345,800 of tax deferred under this provision, reduced by the allowable unified tax credit, will be at a maximum rate of 2%. (See Sec. 6601(j)(2).)

Family Limited Partnerships

General Approach

Gift and estate tax savings on the transfer of a family business may be realized through the use of a family limited partnership (FLP). The typical FLP is initially established by owners wishing to transfer value in the business and future appreciation to the next generation while still retaining control of the business or assets being transferred. To effect these goals the transferor(s) may transfer the assets of the business to a limited partnership receiving a very small general partnership interest and a large limited partnership interest. Gift and estate tax savings can be realized in two ways. First, a systematic giving program, utilizing the annual exclusion, can be established by transferring small amounts of the limited partnership interest to family members each year. Gifts of partnership interests can be made much more efficiently and economically than can undivided interests in real estate or other assets. Second, and more important, these transfers should be subject to control and marketability discounts, allowing interests in assets substantially in excess of the underlying fair market value of those assets to be transferred without gift tax or reduction of the taxpayers' lifetime exclusion equivalent.

EXAMPLE

John and Mary Smith, a married couple, are the sole owners of a business with assets with a value of $3,000,000. John and Mary have two children, both of whom are married. John and Mary transfer the assets to an FLP, with each receiving a 2% general partnership interest and a 48% limited partnership interest. John and Mary now begin a giving program by transferring limited partnership interests to each of the children and their spouses. John and Mary will be able to make gifts of $80,000 each year, free of gift tax consequences, utilizing their annual exclusions. If, however, control and marketability discounts of 33⅓% can be justified, John and Mary could transfer interests in the underlying assets of $120,000 completely free of gift tax or use of lifetime exemption equivalents. Thus, each could transfer 2% of their limited partnership to the children and their spouses each year, and substantial estate savings can be realized. Also, future appreciation related to the underlying assets transferred is removed from the estates of John and Mary. John and Mary retain control of the business through their general partnership interests. Asset valuations should be reviewed each year to ensure that increases in the value of the underlying assets do not increase gift values above the value of the desired transfer.

Relationship to General Partnership Rules

Family limited partnerships are subject to the general partnership rules of Subchapter K of the Internal Revenue Code. Thus, under Sec. 721(a), no gain or loss will be recognized on the transfer of property to the partnership in exchange for the general and limited partnership interests. Care must be taken, however, to avoid the special rule of Sec. 721(b), which could result in gain being recognized if the partnership would be treated as an investment company within the meaning of Sec. 351. Reg. Sec. 1.351-1(c) defines a transfer to an investment company as one that results in the diversification of the transferor's interest and where the transferor is either a regulated investment company, a real estate investment trust, or a corporation more than 80% of whose assets other than cash and nonconvertible debt obligations are held for investment and are readily marketable stocks or securities, or interests in regulated investment companies or real estate investment trusts.

The retention of a general partnership interest may generate some concern over whether the gift of the limited partnership interest can be included in the estate of the transferor under either Sec. 2036 or Sec. 2038. Sec. 2036 requires inclusion if the decedent retained the right to control the use, enjoyment, or income of the transferred property. In a number of private letter rulings (e.g., Ltr. Ruls. 8611004, 9310039, and 9415007) the Internal Revenue Service has ruled that the control of the general partner over the assets does not cause inclusion under this section. Sec. 2038 requires inclusion in the estate if the decedent retains control or the enjoyment of property through a power to alter, amend, revoke, or terminate the transfer. The private letters rulings cited also exempt family limited partnerships from the consequences of this section.

Anti-Abuse Rules

Reg. Sec. 1.701-2 provides anti-abuse rules for the formation and operation of partnerships. This regulation details situations where the IRS will ignore the partnership shell and attribute ownership of assets and income directly to the partners where tax savings rather than sound business purpose is the primary motive for the formation of the partnership. In Announcement

95-8, 1995-7 IRB 56 the service has stated that it will apply this regulation only to income taxes and not to transfer taxes. While this relieves some anxiety as to the treatment of FLPs, it is still important that a sound business purpose be established upon the formation of the FLP. Business purposes that have stood the test of time and review are asset protection against creditors and failed marriages; protection from future creditors; cost savings from having the assets consolidated in one organization; and avoidance of out-of-state probate.

Valuation Discounts

One of the primary tax-planning characteristics of the FLP is the ability to transfer interests in the underlying assets of the FLP at a gift tax value which is substantially less than the actual value of the assets. This is accomplished through the use of control or minority and marketability discounts. Since the limited partner cannot engage in the management of the partnership, the value of that interest would be diminished to a potential buyer. This would be true where the limited partnership interest represented less than a 50% ownership interest, but due to the lack of ability to participate in management, would also seem to apply where the limited interest represented a majority of ownership. While the principle of discounting minority or noncontrolling interests is well established in tax law, the IRS has in the past contended that such discounts were not available in family-controlled situations. The IRS has recently agreed, however, that such discounts are available even though the entire ownership is held by a family unit. (See Rev. Rul. 93-12, 1993-1 C.B. 202.) While this ruling concerns a gift of stock in a closely held corporation, the same principle should apply to FLPs.

Discounts may also be available for lack of marketability. Few buyers will be willing to purchase a limited partnership interest where they have no control over the underlying assets, no control over distributions, and indeed may be unable to sell or withdraw from the business in the future. Withdrawal restrictions could be placed in the partnership agreement to help ensure that such discounts are available. Care should be taken, however, that such restrictions do not violate the provisions of Sec. 2704 which provide that such restrictions will be ignored in valuing an entity if they are more restrictive than those included in federal or state law.

Income Tax Considerations

Family limited partnerships can also be used to transfer taxable income to other family members through gifts of limited partnership interests. However, where partnership interests are given or sold to family members, Sec. 704(e) places restrictions on the allocation of income. First, member(s) (the general partner(s) in the FLP) who provide services to the partnership must receive adequate allocations of income to compensate for those services. Second, once these allocations for services are made, allocations of remaining income must be strictly in accordance with the family members' capital interests. Family members for this purpose are spouses, ancestors, lineal descendants, and trusts established for their benefit.

EXAMPLE

Bill and Sue Jones, husband and wife, each own a 5% general partnership interest and a 45% limited partnership interest in the AB partnership. Bill and Sue each provide services to the partnership valued at $20,000. Bill transfers a 25% limited partnership interest to Billie, a daughter, and Sue transfers a 25% limited partnership interest to Donnie, a son. Net income of the partnership for the year is $90,000. Income of $40,000 must be allocated to Bill and Sue for services provided. Further, the remaining income must be allocated $12,500 each to Bill, Sue, Billie, and Donnie in accordance with the 25% interest each now owns in the partnership.

While FLPs offer substantial benefits in the form of asset protection and tax savings, extreme care should be exercised in the use of this form of organization. In recent months the IRS has mounted an attack on FLPs, particularly where the FLP has been formed shortly before the death of the primary asset owner; where no business purpose can be established; and/or where the primary asset owner was incompetent and the FLP was formed under a power of attorney. The establishment of a sound business purpose is critical if the FLP is to stand up under IRS scrutiny. Also, prudence would seem to dictate that the FLP be established while the primary asset owner is in good health, and, where possible, well in advance of any gift or estate transfers. Also, accountants and/or attorneys with substantial experience in establishing and defending these entities would seem essential.

Relation to Other Provisions

An interest in an FLP can be valued under the special use valuation provisions of Sec. 2032A if all the requirements of this section are met. (See Sec. 2032A(g) and Reg. Sec. 2032A-3.) An interest in a partnership can also be used to qualify for payments on the installment basis under Sec. 6166.

Corporations

Corporate Shares Transferred by Gift

A regular corporation, commonly referred to as a *C corporation,* can be an effective form of organization for the transfer of a family business to the next generation. If a family business is held as a sole proprietorship it is sometimes difficult to transfer small undivided interests in real estate or other assets. If, however, the business is incorporated, shares of stock in any amount can be transferred. Giving programs can be established that allow the transfer of a substantial portion of the value of the business over time, free of gift tax, by using the annual exclusion and/or the lifetime exemption equivalent. As long as less than 50% of the voting stock is transferred, or only nonvoting stock is transferred, the original owner of the business can maintain control while reducing the value to be included in his or her gross estate.

Income tax liability can usually be avoided on such incorporation using Sec. 351 and related provisions.

Gifts of stock representing a minority interest in the corporation will be subject to the same provisions previously described for family limited partnerships and should be subject to valuation discounts similar to those for FLPs. If the stock is not traded on an established exchange, marketability discounts should also be available, as the stock is valued for gift tax purposes. Thus underlying assets may be transferred that represent value substantially in excess of the gift tax value assigned to the transferred stock.

Estate Freezes

A technique that may be effective for the transfer of ownership of a family-owned corporation is the exchange of existing common stock in the corporation for newly issued preferred and common stock, followed by a gift of the common stock to younger members of the family, with the original owners retaining the preferred stock. To be tax-effective the exchange of the common for preferred and common must be structured to meet the requirements of Sec. 368(a)(1)(E) for a recapitalization.

Estate Freezes Before December 18, 1987

Prior to December 18, 1987, transfers of family-owned corporations were usually effected by transferring nonvoting common stock to the younger generation, with voting preferred stock retained by the transferors. The preferred stock was usually accorded dividend and liquidation rights, which gave it value essentially equal to the total value of the enterprise. Therefore little or no value was placed on the common stock, and minimal gift tax liability was incurred on the transfer. All future appreciation of the business would accrue to the common stock and was therefore removed from the estate of the older generation. The preferred stock usually provided for noncumulative dividends, and in practice dividends were rarely paid, further increasing the appreciation accruing to the younger generation.

Effect of Sec. 2036(c)

In 1987 Congress enacted Sec. 2036(c), which required that if "any person holds a substantial interest in an enterprise, and such person in effect transfers after December 17, 1987, property having a disproportionately large share of the potential appreciation in such person's interest in the enterprise while retaining an interest in the income of, or rights in, the enterprise, then the retention of the retained interest shall be considered to be a retention of the enjoyment of the transferred property." This provision caused new plans of the type previously discussed to fail, since retention of the enjoyment of the property triggered inclusion of the transferred property in the transferor's estate under Sec. 2036.

Estate Freezes after October 8, 1990

Sec. 2036(c) was repealed retroactively in 1990. Secs. 2701–2704 were enacted to address transfers such as those just described. Sec. 2701(a) requires special valuation rules where an owner transfers an interest to a family member, with the transferor retaining a preferred right to income. The value of the transferred interest shall be determined by taking the total value of the transferor's interest in the entity and subtracting the value of the applicable retained interest (ARI). Further, the value of the ARI shall be considered to be zero unless it is a distribution right that consists of a right to receive a qualified payment. (See Sec. 2701(a)(3).) Sec. 2701(c)(3) defines a qualified payment as "any dividend payable on a periodic basis under any cumulative preferred stock . . . to the extent that such dividend . . . is determined at a fixed rate." Thus, in the typical estate-freezing arrangement, the preferred stock retained by the transferors must be cumulative if it is to be assigned any value.

Family members for purposes of the aforementioned rules are the spouse of the transferor, a lineal descendent of the transferor or his spouse, and the spouse of such lineal descendent. (See Sec. 2701(c)(1).) The special valuation rules apply only if the transferor and "applicable family members" hold at least 50% of the voting stock or at least 50% of the value of all stock, or the transferor retains a liquidation, put, call, or conversion right. Applicable family members for this purpose are the same as those previously described. (See Sec. 2701(b)(1) and Sec. 2701(c)(1).) The special valuation rules do not apply if market quotations are readily available on an established securities market for the interest retained or the interest transferred, in which case regular valuation rules will apply. (See Sec. 2701(a)(1).) The rules do not apply if the interest transferred and the interest retained are of the same class of stock (i.e., both are common stock) or if the interests differ only in voting rights. Also, the rules do not apply if the retained interest must be exercised at a specific time for a specified amount. (See Sec. 2701(c)(2)(B).)

Reg. Sec. 25.2701-3(b) provides a four-step process for valuing gifts controlled by Sec. 2701:

- *Step 1.* Determine the value of all family-held interests in the entity immediately prior to the transfer, assuming all interests were held by one individual.

- *Step 2.* Subtract from the amount in Step 1 the value of all senior equity (preferred) securities held by the transferor and applicable family members other than the transferee. This value will be zero unless the transferor has a distribution right to a qualified payment (i.e., a cumulative dividend). If the transferor has the right to an extraordinary payment, such as a right to put the securities to the corporation at any time, the value of the securities will be valued at the lower of (1) value of the extraordinary payment or (2) the present value of qualified payments. (See Reg. Sec. 25.2701-2(a)(3).)

- *Step 3.* Allocate the remainder after Step 2 to the transferred interests and other subordinate equity interests held by the transferor and other family members. The amount allocated to the transferred interests, less any adjustments in Step 4, will be the amount of the gift.

- *Step 4.* Reduce the amount determined in Step 3 by allowable minority, marketability, and similar discounts, retained interests, and consideration paid on the transfer.

Reg. Sec. 25.2701-3 provides several examples to illustrate the application of the just-noted valuation rules. The following example is taken from this regulation. Taxpayers and advisors contemplating such transfers should review this regulation for additional information.

EXAMPLE

Corporation X has outstanding 1,000 shares of $1,000 par value preferred stock, each share of which carries a cumulative annual dividend of 8% and a right to put the stock to X for its par value at any time. In addition, there are outstanding 1,000 shares of nonvoting common stock. Party A holds 600 shares of the preferred stock and 750 shares of the common stock. The balance of the preferred and common stock is held by party B, a person unrelated to A. Assume that the right to receive the qualified payment is valued at $800 per share. Because the preferred stock confers both a qualified payment right and an extraordinary payment right, A's rights are valued at the lower of $600,000 (the put right) and $480,000 (the qualified payment right). Assume that the value of A's holdings in X prior to any transfer is determined to be $1,000,000. Party A transfers all of the common stock to C, his child. The amount of the taxable gift to C would be determined as follows:

- *Step 1.* Determine the value of the family holdings in X prior to the transfer, assumed to be $1,000,000.

- *Step 2.* Subtract the value of the preferred stock ($480,000), leaving a residual value of $520,000 for the common stock.

- *Step 3.* Allocate this value to common stock held by the transferee and transferor. Since all the common stock held by A was transferred to B, the entire $520,000 would be allocated to the transferred stock.

- *Step 4.* The amount allocated to the transferred would be reduced by any applicable minority and marketability discounts. The result would be the amount of the taxable gift.

Sec. 2701(a)(4) provides that the minimum value assigned to any junior (common) equity interest must equal at least 10% of the value of all the equity interests in the entity plus any indebtedness of the entity to the transferor.

Where preferred stock with a cumulative dividend is retained in a transfer as previously described, some taxpayers might be inclined to forgo the payment of such dividends in order to allow a larger amount of the business appreciation to accrue to the transferred stock. Sec. 2701(d) provides a remedy for this practice by requiring that the compounded value of any unpaid dividends be included in the value of any subsequent gift of the preferred stock. If the preferred stock is included in the transferor's estate, the estate value must include the compounded value of any unpaid dividends. There is, however, a four-year grace period whereby any dividends paid within four years of the due date are considered as paid on the due date.

Sec. 2701 contains a number of complex provisions concerning the application of the aforementioned rules; unfortunately, these provisions are beyond the scope of this book. Where sizable tax liability could be incurred, an advance revenue ruling will generally be prudent.

Relation to Other Provisions

An interest in a corporation can qualify for special use valuation under Sec. 2032A, where all requirements of this section are met. (See Sec. 2032A(g) and Reg. Sec. 20.2032A-3.) An interest in a corporation can also be used to qualify for installment payments under Sec. 6166.

S Corporations

Introduction

Internal Revenue Code, Subchapter S, Secs. 1361–1379 provide rules for taxation of small corporations (S corporations) and their shareholders that qualify under this subchapter and that elect to be governed by its provisions. With certain exceptions, income of such corporations is not taxed to the corporation but is allocated to the shareholders and reported on their individual income tax returns. These corporations provide the shareholders with certain income tax planning opportunities, but they may prove less useful as a vehicle for passing ownership to children and other family members than do other forms of organization.

Conditions for Election of S Corporation Status

A corporation must be a "small business corporation" to make an election under Subchapter S. Sec. 1361(b) defines a small business corporation as a domestic corporation that is not an ineligible corporation and meets the following criteria:

- Does not have more than 75 shareholders

- Does not have as a shareholder persons other than individuals, estates, certain defined trusts as defined by Sec. 1361(c)(2), and certain tax-exempt organizations as defined by Sec. 1361(c)(7)

- Does not have a nonresident alien as a shareholder

- Does not have more than one class of stock

  Ineligible corporations include:

- Financial institutions that use the reserve method of accounting for bad debts

- Insurance companies

- Corporations with an election in effect under Sec. 936 (relating to the possession tax credit);

- Domestic international sales corporations (DISCs) and former DISCs. (See Sec. 1361(b)(2).)

For purposes of the 75 shareholders rule, husband and wife are treated as one shareholder, and the estate of a deceased spouse and the surviving spouse are treated as a single shareholder. (See Sec. 1361(c)(1).)

An electing small business trust may be a shareholder in an S corporation. The beneficiaries of the trust must be individuals or estates eligible to be S corporation shareholders. However, charitable organizations may hold contingent remainder interests in the S corporation. The beneficiaries must have acquired their interests by gift, bequest, or other nonpurchase acquisition. Each potential current beneficiary of the trust is considered as a shareholder for purposes of the 75 shareholder test. Income of the S corporation attributable to the trust is taxed at 39.6%.

Certain exempt organizations are allowed as shareholders. These organizations include qualified retirement plan trusts under Sec. 401(a) and charitable organizations under Sec. 501(c)(3). Income of the S corporation attributable to the exempt organization is treated as unrelated business income subject to the unrelated business income tax.

An S corporation may own any percentage of a C corporation's stock. However, an S corporation may not join in the filing of a consolidated return with affiliated C corporations. An S corporation may also own a qualified subchapter S subsidiary. A qualified subchapter S subsidiary is any domestic corporation that is an S corporation and is 100% owned by another S corporation. The parent S corporation must elect to treat the subsidiary S corporation as a qualified subchapter S corporation. All of the assets, liabilities, income, expenses, and credits on the parent S corporation and its qualified subchapter S subsidiaries are treated as one corporation for tax purposes.

Authorized but unissued shares of a second class of stock will not result in disqualification. (See Sec. 1361(c)(6).) Differences in voting rights of otherwise identical shares of common stock do not result in treatment as a second class of stock. (See Sec. 1361(c)(4).) Safe harbor rules exist to prevent straight debt from being reclassified as a second class of stock. (See Sec. 1361(c)(5).)

An election to be treated as an S corporation for a taxable year may be made at any time during the preceding taxable year or by the fifteenth day of the third month of that taxable year. (See

Sec. 1362(b)(1).) All persons who hold stock on the day of the election must consent to the election. (See Sec. 1362(a)(2).) Other persons who held stock during a taxable year for which the election is effective but who are not shareholders on the date of the election must also consent to the election. (See Sec. 1362(b)(2).) Where stock is held by a married couple as community property state, each spouse must consent to the election.

Termination of S Corporation Election

Once made, an S corporation election is effective for the year of election and for all succeeding taxable years unless terminated. An election can be terminated in a number of different ways. Shareholders holding a majority of the outstanding shares may voluntarily terminate an election. Such termination is effective for the current taxable year if made before the fifteenth day of the third month of that taxable year; otherwise it is effective for the next taxable year. Shareholders can, however, specify a prospective termination date, in which case the termination will be effective as of that date. (See Sec. 1362(d)(1).) New shareholders do not have to consent to an existing election. However, a new shareholder owning more than 50% of the outstanding stock could terminate an election under this section.

An election will be terminated if the corporation ceases to be a small business corporation (e.g., if a nonresident alien, a corporation, or a partnership should become a shareholder in the corporation). Terminations of this type are effective on the date of the disqualifying event. (See Sec. 1362(d)(2).)

An election will be terminated if an S corporation that has earnings and profits from a time when it was a C (regular) corporation has passive investment income that exceeds 25% of its gross receipts for three consecutive years. Passive investment income for this purpose includes royalties, rents, interest, dividends, annuities, and gains from the sale of stock and securities. An election so terminated becomes effective on the first day of the next taxable year after the three consecutive years of excess passive income. (See Sec. 1326(d)(3).)

An election that is terminated by the corporation ceasing to be a small business corporation or from the passive investment income provisions, and which is determined by the IRS to be inadvertent, can be allowed to continue with IRS permission if (1) the terminating event is corrected within a reasonable period of time and (2) the shareholders agree to adjustments recommended by the IRS. (See Sec. 1362(f).)

Once a termination has occurred, a new election cannot be made until the fifth year that begins after the first taxable year for which the termination is effective. The IRS may consent to an earlier election. (See Sec. 1362(g).) The shareholders of a corporation that terminated an election in the five-year period immediately preceding January 1, 1997, may make a new election without obtaining IRS consent.

When a termination occurs on a date other than on the first day of the taxable year, an allocation of income must be made for that taxable year for the periods prior to and after the termination date. The corporation must file a tax return as an S corporation for the period prior to the termination and a return as a C corporation for the period after the termination. Each item of income and/or expense is allocated to the two periods on a pro rata basis. The corporation may elect to allocate income to the two periods under normal accounting rules, with the consent of all affected shareholders at the time of termination and all other persons who owned stock during the short S corporation year. (See Sec. 1362(e).)

Operating Rules

A detailed description of the operating rules of S corporations is beyond the scope of this book. These rules are contained in Secs. 1363–1379 and can be summarized as follows:

- No income tax liability is incurred by the corporation except for tax on excess net passive income (Sec. 1375), built-in gains (Sec. 1374), and LIFO recapture (Sec. 1363(d)).

- Income, expense, gain, and loss are allocated to the shareholders on a per-share per-day basis. Income, expense, gain, and loss retain their character to the shareholder. Deduction of expenses and losses in excess of income and gains by a shareholder are limited to the shareholder's basis in stock and debt with an indefinite carryover of disallowed losses. (See Sec. 1366.)

- If the corporation has no C corporation accumulated earnings and profits, distributions to shareholders are tax-free to the shareholders to the extent of stock basis. Distributions in excess of basis are recognized as capital gain. If the corporation has C corporation accumulated earnings and profits, distributions are tax-free to the extent of income previously taxed to the shareholder. Distributions in excess of this amount are treated as dividends paid out of earnings and profits with any excess being a return of capital. The corporation may, with the consent of all affected shareholders, elect to treat distributions as first coming from C corporation accumulated earnings and profits. (See Sec. 1368.)

- A shareholder's basis in stock is increased by any income (including tax-exempt income) allocated to the shareholder and by the excess of depletion deductions over the basis of the depletable property. The shareholder's basis is reduced by nontaxable distributions, expenses and losses allocated to the shareholder (including nondeductible expenses), and by depletion on oil and gas property held by the corporation. (See Sec. 1367.)

- An S corporation must generally use a calendar year as its reporting period. There are two exceptions to this general rule. The first exception is for corporations that can establish a natural business year. For this exception, a natural business year is established if 25% or more of the gross receipts occur in the last two months of such year for three consecutive years. As a second exception, corporations may elect or change to a fiscal year that does not result in deferral of income to the share-holders of more than the greater of three months or the defer-ral period of the year from which the change is being made. If this election is made, the corporation must make a non-interest-bearing deposit with the IRS roughly equal to the tax being deferred by the shareholders from use of the fiscal year. (See Sec. 444.)

Income Tax Planning

The S corporation offers a number of income tax planning advantages over the regular corporation while retaining some of the advantages of the C corporation such as limited liability, free transferability of interest, and continuity of life.

- With the exceptions discussed previously there is only a sin-gle level of income tax on corporate income.

- Losses can be passed through to the shareholders. This is espe-cially beneficial to new businesses, which may incur substan-tial losses in the early years of their existence. C corporation losses can only be used through carrybacks and carryovers. For new businesses, this may mean a wait of several years before such losses can be utilized. In the S corporation care must be taken to ensure that shareholders maintain a basis in their stock sufficient to absorb pass-through losses. Otherwise these losses will be carried over, and full benefit of the losses may not be realized until future periods.

- Mature corporations that are generating substantial amounts of cash may also use the S election to avoid problems with the accumulated earnings tax. For such corporations the election will also reduce the tax cost when excess cash is paid out to the shareholders, because dividends paid by S corporations are usually tax-free to the shareholders.

- S corporations can also be used to allocate business income to family members in lower tax brackets. Since income is allo-cated based on the percentage of shares held by each shareholder, the transfer of shares by gift to family members in lower tax brackets can result in substantial tax savings. Care must be taken, however, to avoid the reallocation rules of Sec. 1366(e). This section gives the IRS authority to reallocate income to family members providing services to the corporation for which they have not been reasonably compensated. It is essential that documentation be developed and maintained to verify that all senior family members providing services have been adequately compensated. Present IRS practice indicates that this section will be rigidly enforced.

- The alternative minimum tax does not apply to S corporations, thus avoiding the complex adjusted current earnings adjustment and the related potential for increased tax liability to which C corporations are subject. Certain income and expense items passed through to shareholders may, however, impact the shareholder's individual alternative minimum tax.

Estate Planning

While the S corporation can be a useful vehicle for income tax planning, its use in estate planning is limited. The one-class-of-stock restriction prevents the use of the estate freeze methodology previously discussed. Also, the limitations on the type of persons who can be shareholders in an S corporation prevent the use of trusts and partnerships as vehicles for the transfer of ownership of the corporation. A gifting program similar to that previously discussed for C corporation stock can be undertaken with S corporation stock. As with the C corporation, substantial amounts of wealth can be transferred with a well-structured program. Since differences in voting rights of stock in an S corporation will not destroy the election, nonvoting shares can be transferred to children, with the original holders of the stock retaining control with voting shares.

Stock interests in S corporations can be valued using the special-use valuation methods of Sec. 2032A if the underlying property and the decedent and transferee family members meet all the requirements of this section. (See Sec. 2032A(g) and Reg. Sec. 20.2032A-3.)

An interest in an S corporation can be an interest in a closely held business and can be used to qualify the estate for installment payment under Sec. 6166 if all the conditions of this section are met. (See Sec. 6166(b)(2)(C).)

Valuation of gifts of minority interests of S corporation stock should be subject to minority and marketable discounts in a manner similar to that for interest in C corporations and FLPs.

Limited Liability Companies

Limited liability companies (LLC) are a relatively new phenomenon in the world of business organization. All 50 states now permit the formation of LLCs. These companies offer businesses the best characteristics of both corporations and partnerships. These companies offer limited liability to owners, much like a corporation does, and a pass-through of income to owners, much like a partnership does. However, unlike a partnership, LLCs do not require the existence of a general partner. While S corporations offer these same advantages, they are limited by the 75-shareholder rule and restrictions on the type of shareholders allowed. LLCs are not generally subject to these restrictions. Limited liability is provided by statute. Partnership treatment for tax purposes is accomplished by not electing corporate treatment under the "check-the-box" regulations under Sec. 7701. (See Reg. Sec. 301.7701-3.)

For income tax planning purposes, LLCs offer essentially the same opportunities as do limited partnerships. For estate planning purposes, logic would indicate that many of the same procedures used with FLPs would also be appropriate for LLCs. However, until the administrative and case law is more fully developed it would seem prudent to approach the use of LLCs with some caution.

Worksheet 4.1 Computation Aid Transfer of a Closely Held Business

Qualification for Special Use Valuation Under Sec. 2032A

50% Real and Personal Property Test

Real and personal property of the farm and/or closely
held business realty _____

Less: Unpaid mortgages or indebtedness with respect to
such property _____

Equals: Adjusted value of such property   A _____

Gross Estate (including closely held property at best use) _____

Less: Unpaid mortgages or indebtedness with
respect to property included in the gross estate _____

Add: Gifts made during last 3 years _____

Equals: Adjusted gross estate under Sec. 2032A _____

50% of adjusted gross value of estate   B _____

Does A exceed or equal B? If so, 50% test is met. _____

25% Qualified Real Property Test

Qualified real property (i.e., farmland), for qualified use,
of the farm and/or closely held business realty _____

Less: Unpaid mortgages or indebtedness with respect
to such property _____

Equals: Adjusted value of such property   C _____

Adjusted gross value of the estate (above) _____

25% of adjusted gross value of estate   D _____

Does C exceed or equal D? If so, 25% test is met. _____

Worksheet 4.2 Computation Aid Transfer of a Closely Held Business

Checklist for Attachments for Special Use Valuation Under Sec. 2032A

Sec. 2032A-8(a)(3) provides that an election under Sec. 2032A is made by (1) attaching the agreement, described in paragraph (c)(1) of that section, to a timely filed estate tax return, and (2) a notice of election containing the following 14 items of information:

1. The decedent's name and taxpayer identification number as they appear on the estate tax return

2. The relevant qualified use

3. The items of real property shown on the estate tax return to be specially valued pursuant to the election (identified by schedule and item number)

4. The fair market value of the real property to be specially valued under Sec. 2032A and its value based on its qualified use (both values determined without regard to the adjustments provided by Sec. 2032A(b)(3)(B)

5. The adjusted value (as defined in Sec. 2032A(b)(3)(B)) of all real property which is used in a qualified use and which passes from the decedent to a qualified heir and the adjusted value of all real property to be specially valued

6. The items of personal property shown on the estate tax return that pass from the decedent to a qualified heir and are used in a qualified use under Sec. 2032A (identified by schedule and item number) and the total value of such personal property adjusted as provided under Sec. 2032A(b)(3)(B)

7. The adjusted value of the gross estate, as defined in Sec. 2032a(b)(3)(A)

8. The method used in determining the special value based on use

9. Copies of written appraisals of the fair market value of the real property

10. A statement that the decedent and/or a member of his or her family has owned all specially valued real property for at least 5 years of the 8 years immediately preceding the date of the decedent's death

11. Any periods during the 8-year period preceding the date of the decedent's death during which the decedent or a member of his or her family did not own the property, use it in a qualified use, or materially participate in the operation of the farm or other business within the meaning of Sec. 2032A(e)(6)

Worksheet 4.2 Computation Aid Transfer
of a Closely Held Business (*continued*)

Checklist for Attachments for Special Use Valuation Under Sec. 2032A

12. The name, address, taxpayer identification number, and relationship to the decedent of each person taking an interest in each item of specially valued property, and the value of the property interests passing to each such person based on both fair market value and qualified use

13. Affidavits describing the activities constituting material participation and the identity of the material participant or participants

14. A legal description of the specially valued property

Worksheet 4.3   Computation Aid Transfer
of a Closely Held Business

Method for Valuing Farm(s) for Special Use Valuation Under Sec. 2032A

Average annual gross cash rental for last 5 years   _____

Less: Average annual state and local real estate taxes   _____

Equals: Average annual net cash rental   _____

Divide by: Average annual effective interest rate
for all new Federal Land Bank loans (i.e., 10.5% or 0.105)   _____

Equals: Valuation of land under formula   _____

Value at best use   _____

Sec. 2032A reduction (maximum allowed—$750,000)   _____

Special use value   _____

Sec. 2032A(e)(7)(A) and Reg. Sec. 2032A-4

Worksheet 4.4   Computation Aid Transfer of a Closely Held Business

Qualification for Closely Held Business Deduction Under Sec. 2057

Gross estate   _____

Less:

Claims against the estate   _____

Unpaid mortgages or indebtedness with
   respect to property of the decedent   _____   _____

Plus:

Gifts to family members (other than spouse)
   held continuously by members of the family
   and excludible due to the annual exclusion   _____

Taxable gifts to family members (other than spouse)
   held continuously by members of the family and
   made by the decedent after December 31, 1976
   other than gifts that are includable in the estate   _____

Other gifts made by the decedent within
   3 years of the date of death (other than gifts
   excludible under Sec. 2503(b))   _____

Transfers from the decedent to the decedent's
   spouse within 10 years of the date of death   _____   _____

Adjusted gross estate under Sec. 2057   _____

Multiply by 50% (0.5)   E _____

Qualified family-owned business interests   _____

Plus: Gifts to family members (other than spouse)
   held continuously by members of the family   _____

Less: Debts of estate other than mortgages
   on principal residence, educational or medical
   loans, or other indebtedness up to $10,000   _____   F _____

Does F exceed or equal E? If so, Sec. 2057 test is met.   _____

Worksheet 4.5 Computation Aid Transfer of a Closely Held Business

Amount of Increase in Unified Credit Due to Closely Held Business Deduction Under Sec. 2057

The 1998 Act converts the qualified family-owned business exclusion into a deduction. The deduction for qualified family-owned business interest may not exceed $675,000. (See Sec. 2057(a)(2).) If the estate includes less than $675,000 of qualified family-owned business interests, the applicable exclusion amount is increased on a dollar-for-dollar basis up to the applicable exclusion amount generally available for the year of death. (See Sec. 2057(a)(3)(B).)

Total reduction amount of the gross estate (qualified
family-owned business interest deduction and
applicable exemption amount) $1,300,000

Less: Qualified family-owned business interest (if less
than $675,000; otherwise may elect to use $675,000
or amount applicable to the year of death below) _____

Potential applicable exemption amount _____

Applicable exemption amount (cannot exceed amounts
below based on year of death) _____

Year	Applicable exemption amount	Business deduction amount
1997	$ 600,000	None
1998	625,000	$675,000
1999	650,000	650,000
2000 and 2001	675,000	625,000
2002 and 2003	700,000	600,000
2004	850,000	450,000
2005	950,000	350,000
2006 and after	1,000,000	300,000

Worksheet 4.6 Computation Aid Transfer of a Closely Held Business

Qualification for Installment Payment of Tax Under Sec. 6166

Qualification test

Gross estate   _____

Less:

Funeral expenses   _____

Administration expenses   _____

Claims against the estate   _____

Unpaid mortgages or indebtedness with respect
     to property of the decedent   _____

Income taxes on income received after
     the decedent's death   _____

Other deductions under Sec. 2053   _____

Deductible losses under Sec. 2054   _____   _____

Adjusted gross estate under Sec. 6166   _____

Multiply by 35% (0.35)   G _____

Value of interest in closely held business
     included in gross estate   H _____

Does H exceed or equal G? If so, Sec. 6166
     test is met.   _____

Amount of taxes deferred

Value of interest in closely held business
     included in gross estate   _____

Divided by: Adjusted gross estate under Sec. 6166   _____

Equals: Proportion of taxes deferred   _____

CHAPTER

5

Estate Planning

A Quick Overview of the Transfer Tax System

Estate planning is a process that involves much more than the minimization of estate taxes. Small estates probably do not require any tax avoidance planning. Very large estates may require a level of tax planning that is beyond the scope of this book. We will attempt to provide some general guidance that will be helpful for all estates and some basic estate planning techniques that will apply for medium and larger estates.

The United States has a unified system that taxes transfers of property during an individual's lifetime (gifts) and property transferred as a result of the individual's death. The system is structured so that the sum of an individual's taxable gifts and net assets transferred at death must exceed an applicable exemption amount before any gift or estate taxes are imposed. The applicable exemption amount will be $1,000,000 when completely phased in after the year 2005.

Under prior law, the unified credit of $192,800 exempted the first $600,000 of cumulative transfers at death and through gifts.

The unified credit under prior law was replaced in 1997 by an applicable credit amount for decedents dying and gifts made after 1997. The applicable credit amount is the amount of the tentative transfer tax that would be offset equal to the transfer taxes computed for the applicable exemption amount. The phase-in schedule for the applicable unified credit amounts and applicable exemption amounts appears in Table 5.1, and the unified transfer tax rate schedule appears in Table 5.2.

Consequently, for a decedent dying in 2006 or later with a net estate of $2,000,000 and no taxable gifts, the net transfer tax payable would be $335,000, computed as follows:

Tentative tax—	
using unified transfer tax rate schedule	$780,800
Less: applicable unified credit—	
transfer tax on $1,000,000	$345,800
Net transfer tax payable	$335,000

Note that $1,000,000 of net estate is exempted from tax, but the marginal tax rate on the first dollar over $1,000,000 is 41%.

In addition, a surtax of 5% on cumulative taxable transfers between $10,000,000 and the amount at which the average tax rate

TABLE 5.1 Phase-In of Unified Credit
and Applicable Exemption Amount

	Applicable unified credit	Applicable exemption amount
1997	$192,800	$ 600,000
1998	202,050	625,000
1999	211,300	650,000
2000 and 2001	220,550	675,000
2002 and 2003	229,800	700,000
2004	287,300	850,000
2005	326,300	950,000
2006 and after	345,800	1,000,000

TABLE 5.2 Unified Transfer Tax Rate Schedule

Sum of taxable estate and adjusted taxable gifts		Tentative tax
Over	**But not over**	
$-0-	$10,000	18% of such amount
$10,000	$20,000	$1,800 plus 20% of excess over $10,000
$20,000	$40,000	$3,800 plus 22% of excess over $20,000
$40,000	$60,000	$8,200 plus 24% of excess over $40,000
$60,000	$80,000	$13,000 plus 26% of excess over $60,000
$80,000	$100,000	$18,200 plus 28% of excess over $80,000
$100,000	$150,000	$23,800 plus 30% of excess over $100,000
$150,000	$250,000	$38,800 plus 32% of excess over $150,000
$250,000	$500,000	$70,800 plus 34% of excess over $250,000
$500,000	$750,000	$155,800 plus 37% of excess over $500,000
$750,000	$1,000,000	$248,300 plus 39% of excess over $750,000
$1,000,000	$1,250,000	$345,800 plus 41% of excess over $1,000,000
$1,250,000	$1,500,000	$448,300 plus 43% of excess over $1,250,000
$1,500,000	$2,000,000	$555,800 plus 45% of excess over $1,500,000
$2,000,000	$2,500,000	$780,800 plus 49% of excess over $2,000,000
$2,500,000	$3,000,000	$1,025,800 plus 53% of excess over $2,500,000
$3,000,000		$1,290,800 plus 55% of excess over $3,000,000

is 55% is added to phase out the benefit of the graduated rates and the unified credit. Committee reports indicate that transfers before the effective date of the phaseout provision (January 1988) will be included in the cumulative transfers subject to the surtax. If cumulative transfers in excess of $21,040,000 were made prior to the effective date, future transfers are not subject to the surtax.

The Gift Tax

The gift tax is imposed on a calendar year basis on transfers of property by gift by any individual. (See Sec. 2501.) It is cumulative during an individual's life. The gift tax is the excess of a tentative tax, computed on the aggregate sum of the taxable gifts for the calendar year and the preceding calendar years, over a tentative tax computed on the aggregate sum of the taxable gifts for the preceding calendar years. (See Sec. 2502(a).) The tax is computed with the same tax rates used for estate purposes in Sec. 2001(c). This computation is illustrated with the gift tax formula that follows.

Computation of the Gift Tax: Gift Tax Formula

Start with:	Aggregate amount of gifts for the current period (Sec. 2501 and 2511)
Less:	One-half of above amount of gifts to third parties, if taxpayer and spouse elect gift-splitting (Sec. 2513)
Plus:	One-half of gifts made by spouse to third parties, if gift-splitting is elected
Less:	Annual exclusion of $10,000 (or amount adjusted for inflation for years after 1998) per donee per year for all gifts of present interests (Sec. 2523)
Less:	Charitable contribution deduction (Sec. 2522)
Less:	Marital deduction for qualifying gifts to spouse (Sec. 2523)
Equals:	Taxable gifts for the period
Plus:	Amount of taxable gifts for prior periods (Sec. 2504)
Equals:	Total taxable gifts
Compute:	Tax on taxable gifts (Sec. 2001(c))
Less:	Tax, at present rates, on total taxable gifts made in prior periods (Sec. 2001(c))

Equals: Tax on current period's gifts (Sec. 2502)

Less: Amount of maximum applicable unified credit amount for this year, reduced by amount of credit previously utilized (Sec. 2505)

Equals: Gift taxes payable for current period

COMPUTATION AID: For a worksheet to compute the estimated gift tax, see Worksheet 5.1 on page 170.

Transfers Treated as Gifts

The gift tax is generally imposed on all transfers in trust or otherwise, direct or indirect, of real or personal and tangible or intangible property. (See Sec. 2511.) Regulations under Sec. 2511 detail the transfers included in and excluded from treatment as gifts.

Section 2501 specifically excludes certain transfers of intangible property by a nonresident not a citizen of the United States and transfers to political organizations.

Section 2503(e) excludes certain transfers for education expenses or medical expenses from characterization as gifts. The amounts so expended must be paid directly to an education organization for the education or training of the donee or to a person providing medical care of the donee.

Section 2516 excludes transfers made to a husband or wife in settlement of marital or property rights or to provide a reasonable allowance for the support of issue of the marriage during minority.

The Annual Exclusion

In defining the term *taxable gifts,* Sec. 2503 allows for an annual exclusion of $10,000 for gifts to any number of persons each year. After 1998 the amount of the annual exclusion will be indexed annually for inflation in increments of $1,000.

Gifts of a future interest do not generally qualify for the exclusion. However, transfers for the benefit of individuals under the age of 21 will not be considered transfers of a future interest if the property and the income therefrom may be expended by, or for the benefit of, the donee before attainment of the age of 21, and any amounts not so expended will pass to the donee upon that donee's twenty-first birthday. (See Sec. 2503(c).)

This exclusion allows for the transfer of substantial property over a period of years without the imposition of either the gift or estate tax. For example, an individual with five children can transfer $50,000 per year to his or her children. A couple electing gift-splitting under Sec. 2513 can transfer $100,000 per year to five children with no gift or estate tax liability. These amounts should increase due to the annual exclusion inflation adjustments for gifts made after 1998. A gift-giving program can result in the transfer of large amounts of property over several years with no gift or estate tax implications.

The Marital Deduction

A donor spouse is allowed an unlimited deduction for lifetime gifts made to his or her spouse. (See Sec. 2523.) This allows for gifts between spouses with no gift or estate tax implications.

Certain terminable interests—interests that will terminate after a certain period or on the occurrence of some event—do not qualify for the marital deduction. (See Sec. 2523.) However, if a life estate meets the requirements of Sec. 2523(f), it may qualify for the marital deduction if it is *qualified terminable interest property*. Property is qualified terminable interest property (QTIP) if the following conditions apply:

- The donee spouse is entitled to the income from the property for life.

- Income from the property is payable to the donee spouse at least annually.

- No person has the power to appoint any part of the property to any person other than the donee spouse.

■ An irrevocable election to have all or part of the trust qualify for the marital deduction is made by the donor and attached to the gift tax return. (See Sec. 2523.)

Charitable Contribution Deduction

The value of gifts to charities is allowed as a deduction in computing taxable gifts. (See Sec. 2522.) Unlike income tax treatment of charitable contributions, there is no limit on the amount of the gift tax deduction for contributions to charitable organizations. In addition to the gift tax deduction, these gifts result in a charitable contribution for income tax purposes.

Gifts to charities often take the form of a *charitable remainder trust* or a *charitable lead trust.* The charitable remainder trust gives the income from the property to a noncharitable beneficiary, with the remainder passing to the charity after the noncharitable beneficiary has enjoyed the income for life or for a term of years. A charitable lead trust gives the income to a charity, with the remainder passing to a noncharitable beneficiary. In order to qualify for the gift tax charitable contribution deduction, the gift must meet the requirements of Sec. 2522, which requires that the trust be a charitable remainder annuity trust, a charitable remainder unitrust, a pooled income fund, an income interest in a trust in the form of a guaranteed annuity or fixed percentage of the value of the property, or an interest described in Sec. 170(f)(3)(B). Section 170(f)(3)(B) refers to a remainder interest in a personal residence or a farm, an undivided portion of a person's entire interest in property, or a qualified conservation contribution.

A charitable remainder annuity trust is a trust from which a fixed amount, not less than 5% of the initial net fair market value of the property placed in trust, is to be paid at least annually to one or more persons, one of which is a qualifying charity. A charitable remainder unitrust is a trust from which a fixed percentage, not less than 5% of the net fair market value of its assets valued annually, is to be paid at least annually to one or more persons, one of which is a qualifying charity. (See Sec. 664.) A pooled income fund is a trust to which each donor transfers property, contributing an irrevocable remainder interest in such property to or for the use of a qualifying charity, and retaining an income interest for the life of one or more beneficiaries. (See Sec. 642(c)(5).)

The Tax Relief Act of 1997 added two additional limitations for charitable remainder trusts. The present value of the remainder interest for any transfer to a charitable remainder trust must equal at least 10% of the net value of the property transferred, computed on the date of the transfer. For a charitable remainder annuity trust, the value of the remainder interest must be at least 10% of the initial value of all property placed in the trust. For a charitable remainder unitrust, the 10% minimum applies to each contribution of property to the trust. This provision generally applies to transfers after July 28, 1997. It will not apply to transfers under a will executed on or before July 28, 1997, if the decedent dies before January 1, 1999, without having republished the will or amending it by codicil or if the decedent was, on July 18, 1997, mentally incompetent and did not regain competency before dying. (See Sec. 664(d)(1); Act Sec. 1089(b)(6)(B).)

In addition, a trust will not qualify as a charitable remainder trust if the required annual payout to the income beneficiary is greater than 50% of the value of the trust's assets. For a charitable remainder annuity trust, the annual payout cannot exceed 50% of the initial value of the trust's assets. For a charitable remainder unitrust, the annual payout cannot exceed 50% of the value of the trust's assets as determined annually. This provision applies to transfers June 18, 1997. (See Sec. 664(d)(2).)

The value of the remainder interest is determined under Sec. 7520, using 120% of the federal midterm rate. Current rates are published by most tax services and are posted on the IRS Web Page at http://www.irs.ustreas.gov. Present value factors are contained in Reg. Sec. 20.2031-7.

EXAMPLE

Mrs. Graves transfers $800,000 of property to a charitable remainder annuity trust. She retains an annual annuity of $56,000 for life, with the remaining property to be transferred to the American Heart Association at her death. Mrs. Graves is 60 years old at the time of the gift. If the factor were based upon an interest rate of 6%, the resulting interest rate would be 7.2% when multiplied by 120%. The single-life remainder factor using age 60 and 7.2% is .31317. (See Reg. Sec. 20.2031-7, Table S.) The remainder interest is computed as follows.

Total amount transferred to trust		$800,000
Less: value of retained interest		
Annuity payment	$56,000	
X annuity factor		
(1.0 − .31317)/7.2%	9.539	$534,201
Remainder interest		$265,799

    On Mrs. Graves's gift tax return, the gift to the American Heart Association of $265,799 is offset by the gift tax deduction of the same amount. She is also entitled to a charitable contribution deduction of $265,799 on her personal income tax return.

Advantages of Gifts Over Transfers at Death

- The payment of gift taxes reduces the amount of property to be transferred by an individual. The payment of estate taxes does not reduce the amount included in the taxable estate.

- The appreciation in the value of the property from the date of the gift until the donor's death escapes the transfer tax.

- Thoughtful use of the annual exclusion can result in substantial transfers with no transfer tax implications. There is no corresponding provision in the estate tax law.

Disadvantages of Gifts

- The person making the gift may find that he or she gave away too much and that the assets should have been kept for living expenses.

- The person receiving the gift generally has a basis in the property equal to the donor's basis (except in the case where the donor's basis exceeded the property's value upon the date of the gift and the donee is disposing of the property at a loss). If the property passed to the person as a result of inheritance, the basis would be the property's value on the date of death (or the alternate valuation date if elected by the executor). If the asset has been increasing in value and the donee/heir eventually disposes of the property, property received as a gift will result in a larger gain than property received as an inheritance.

Valuation Issues

A gift is valued, for gift tax purposes and for eventual inclusion in the estate tax computation, at its value on the date of the gift. Small blocks of publicly traded stock or real estate in a relatively stable market can be valued using conventional methods. However, the perceptive tax planner should consider any applicable discount when valuing gifts. Discounts that have been successfully applied included:

- Declining or already unfavorable market conditions
- Lack of voting rights
- Minority interest
- Lack of marketability for ownership of a fractional interest
- The value of high annuity payments to the grantor of a grantor retained annuity trust

A reliable, professional appraisal is extremely important. This appraisal provides support if the gift tax return is questioned. The IRS has been successful in revaluing gifts for gift tax purposes and even for estate tax purposes upon eventual examination of the estate tax return. The Taxpayer Relief Act passed in 1997 contained a provision to prevent revaluation of prior gifts for estate tax purposes in certain cases. For gifts made after August 5, 1997, if the value of the gift has been shown on a gift tax return with proper disclosure and the statute of limitations for the gift tax return has run, the gifts may not be revalued for estate tax purposes. (See Sec. 2001(f); P. L. 105-34.)

The Estate Tax

The Gross Estate

The gross estate generally includes the value of all of the assets owned by the decedent at the date of death. (See Sec. 2031.) The executor may elect to value the property at its value six months after the date of death if such alternate valuation decreases both the gross estate and the estate tax. (See Sec. 2032.) This valuation is generally straightforward, involving an appraisal or other valuation method, such as prices quoted in the *Wall Street Journal* for stocks.

It is generally simple to determine what assets were owned by the decedent at death. If the estate is required to go through probate, the executor will have to inventory the assets owned by the decedent. However, some types of assets are treated differently for estate tax purposes.

Life insurance paid to the estate is included. Life insurance paid to other beneficiaries is also included if the decedent possessed any of the incidents of ownership at death. (See Sec. 2042.) In addition, gifts of life insurance within three years of the date of death will result in the inclusion of the value of the policies in the decedent's estate. (See Sec. 2035.)

When property has been gifted but the right to the income, possession, or enjoyment of the property has been retained, the value of the property is included in the gross estate. (See Sec. 2036.) The property is also included if the decedent retained the right to alter, amend, revoke, or terminate the gift. (See Sec. 2038.)

Some or all of the value of jointly owned property is included in the gross estate. The decedent's share of the property is included, depending upon the type of joint ownership. (See Sec. 2033.)

If the decedent was the surviving spouse of a decedent that elected to have property treated as qualified terminable interest property under Sec. 2056, that remaining property is now included in the surviving spouse's estate. (See Sec. 2044.) This is also true of gifts received as qualified terminable interest property under Sec. 2523.

Property for which the decedent had a general power of appointment is included in the gross estate. This is true even if the power was never exercised. (See Sec. 2041.)

The value of an annuity receivable by a beneficiary by reason of surviving the decedent is included in the gross estate. (See Sec. 2039.) This would include annuities resulting from a qualified pension plan.

The value of curtesy or dower rights of the surviving spouse is included in the decedent's estate. This is also true of rights to an estate in lieu of dower or curtesy created by statute. (See Sec. 2034.)

Certain qualified real property can be valued on the basis of its actual use value rather than its value as determined by its highest and best use. (See Sec. 2032A.) This should be considered for farms and other closely held business activities. See "Sole Proprietorship in an Estate: Special Use Valuation" section in Chapter 4 of this book for a full discussion of this provision.

The Tax Relief Act of 1997 and the IRS Restructuring and Reform Act of 1998 contained provisions that allow for the deduction of part of the value of a closely held family business from the gross estate. (See Sec. 2057.) This provision should also be considered for farms and other closely held business activities. See the "Sole Proprietorship: Family-Owned Business Deduction" section in Chapter 4 of this book for a full discussion of this provision.

Reductions in the Gross Estate

The taxable estate is the gross estate as reduced by deductions allowed by Sec. 2053. The deductions include:

- Funeral expenses.
- Administration expenses.

- Claims against the estate.

- Unpaid mortgages, or other indebtedness related to property included in the gross estate.

- Uncompensated losses incurred during the settlement of the estate arising from fires, storms, shipwrecks, or other casualties, or from theft. (See Sec. 2054.)

The Marital Deduction

An estate is allowed an unlimited deduction for the value of property passing to his or her surviving spouse. (See Sec. 2056.) As with the gift tax, this allows property to pass to surviving spouses with no gift or estate tax implications.

Certain terminable interests—interests that will terminate after a certain period or on the occurrence of some event—do not qualify for the marital deduction. (See Sec. 2056.) However, if a life estate meets the requirements of Sec. 2056(b)(7), it may qualify for the marital deduction if it is *qualified terminable interest property*. Property is qualified terminable interest property if the following conditions apply:

- The surviving spouse is entitled to the income from the property for life.

- Income from the property is payable to the surviving spouse at least annually.

- No person has the power to appoint any part of the property to any person other than the surviving spouse.

- An irrevocable election to have all or part of the trust qualify for the marital deduction is made by the executor and attached to the estate tax return. (See Sec. 2056.)

Charitable Deduction

A deduction is allowed for the value of property transferred to certain governmental, charitable, or religious organizations.

These provisions are similar to the income tax provisions covering charitable contributions. (See Sec. 2055.) Directions to make the contributions must be contained in the will of the deceased. The executor cannot make the charitable donation.

Computation of the Estate Tax: Estate Tax Formula

Start with:	Gross estate, valued at date of death or alternate valuation date (Secs. 2013–2046)
Less:	Debts, administrative and funeral expenses, and losses (Secs. 2053–2054)
Less:	Charitable contribution deduction (Sec. 2055)
Less:	Marital Deduction (Sec. 2056)
Equals:	Taxable Estate
Plus:	Adjusted taxable gifts, valued at date-of-gift values (Sec. 2001)
Equals:	Tax base
Compute:	Tentative tax on tax base (Sec. 2001(c))
Less:	Gift taxes paid on post-1976 taxable gifts (Sec. 2001(b))
Less:	Applicable unified credit (Sec. 2010)
Less:	Credit for state death taxes (Sec. 2011)
Less:	Credit for pre-1977 gift tax on transfers included in gross estate (Sec. 2012)
Less:	Credit for tax on prior transfers (Sec. 2013)
Less:	Credit for foreign death taxes (Sec. 2014)
Equals:	Balance due

COMPUTATION AID: For a worksheet to compute the estimated estate tax, see worksheet 5.2 on page 171.

Additional Tax Due on Excess Retirement Accumulation

The additional 15% estate tax imposed on an excess retirement accumulation was repealed for decedents dying after December 31, 1996. (See Sec. 4980A; P. L. 105-34.)

The Generation-Skipping Transfer Tax

To remove the benefit of transferring property to grandchildren or otherwise skipping the estate or gift tax that will be paid by the immediately following generation, a generation-skipping transfer tax is imposed at a flat 55% rate on generation-skipping transfers. The most common generation-skipping transfers are direct transfers from a grandparent to a grandchild and life estates from the grandparent to the child with the remainder interest to the grandchild. Generation-skipping transfers are defined in Sec. 2603. These transfers include taxable distributions, taxable terminations, and direct skips.

A *taxable distribution* is a distribution to a transferee who is a member of a generation at least two generations younger than the transferor. The amount received is subject to the tax. (See Sec. 2611.) The tax is paid by the transferee. (See Sec. 2603.)

A *taxable termination* is the termination by death, lapse of time, release of power, or similar event of an interest held in trust that passes to a transferee who is a member of a generation at least two generations younger than the transferor. The value of the property in which the interest terminates is subject to the tax. (See Sec. 2611.) The tax is paid by the trustee. (See Sec. 2603.)

A *direct skip* is a transfer of property to, or for the benefit of, persons two or more generations below the transferor. The value of the property transferred is subject to the tax. (See Sec. 2611.) The tax is paid by the transferor. (See Sec. 2603.)

There is a lifetime generation-skipping tax exemption of $1 million per grantor. (See Sec. 2631.) This amount will be indexed for inflation for decedents dying and gifts made after 1998. (See Code Sec. 2631(c).)

Basic Goals of Estate Planning

The primary goal of estate planning is to arrange one's affairs so that one's assets are preserved and received by the proper individuals. The reduction of estate and inheritance taxes is an important part of this goal, but it is by no means the only goal of estate planning. The tax advisor should be aware of the many implications of assisting a client in estate planning.

In addition to being sensitive to the client's possible reluctance to discuss his or her own death, a tax advisor would be well advised to remember that the assets being discussed are usually the result of a lifetime of hard work. The emotional impact of deciding upon the disposition of an asset often outweighs the economic impact of its disposition.

Basics of an Estate Plan

Every adult individual should consider acquiring the basics of an estate plan. These basics include the following:

- A will

- A durable power of attorney

- An advance directive to physician

In addition, serious consideration should be given to creating a revocable trust.

A Will

A will is necessary to specify the disposition of property upon death and, for parents of minor children, to name the guardians of the children in the event of both parents' deaths. The laws of the various states will dictate how each of these responsibilities is carried out if an individual dies without a will. This may result in some undesirable outcomes. For example, many state laws divide the decedent's estate between the surviving spouse and the couple's children. In many cases, the client may prefer that all of the estate go to the surviving spouse or be placed in trust with the income to benefit the surviving spouse. A will can accomplish this result.

A Durable Power of Attorney

A durable power of attorney names a conservator and guardian in case of the individual's incapacity. If an individual becomes incapacitated or incompetent without having executed a durable power of attorney, there must be a judicial determination of incapacity, and the court must name the conservator and guardian.

An Advance Directive to Physician

An advance directive to physician, also known as a *living will,* allows an individual to direct that his or her life not be artificially prolonged in the case of a terminal medical condition or persistent unconsciousness. This document serves to provide evidence of the individual's intention so that these decisions can be made after the individual is unable to make his or her intentions known.

Revocable Trusts

Revocable trusts, also known as *living trusts,* have become quite popular as devices to avoid probate costs. Since the trust is revocable, the assets are included in the individual's estate and the income is included in the individual's taxable income. A revocable trust should be considered, but may not be recommended for every client. The advantages of a revocable trust include:

- Probate is avoided for assets placed in the trust. Upon the individual's death, the trustee maintains or distributes the assets in the trust as specified by the trust agreement. There is no need for a probate court to oversee the maintenance and distribution of the assets. If probate costs are great, a revocable trust can result in substantial savings. In addition, the trust agreement is not public record. Probate records are public. Some clients might find this privacy appealing.

- The trust can operate in the event of the individual's incapacity during his or her lifetime. If properly drafted, the trust agreement can allow for the trustee to take over management of the individual's affairs based upon some specific proof of incompetence such as a letter from the individual's physician. The agreement can also specify a trustee of the individual's choosing. This is a much simpler process than most states' legal proceedings required to declare an individual incompetent and to have a guardian appointed.

The disadvantages of a revocable trust include:

- The costs of creating and maintaining a revocable trust may exceed the cost of probating a will. Probate costs in the individual's state of residence should be determined in order to evaluate the relative cost of a will versus a revocable trust. Assets owned jointly pass directly to the other owner with no need for probate. Assets such as life insurance proceeds or an IRA paid to a named beneficiary do not require probate. It is possible that there are very few assets subject to probate.

- Any assets owned by the individual but not placed in the trust will be subject to the probate law. For most individuals, the record-keeping requirements of keeping all of their assets in the trust may be a burden. A common problem with these trusts is that the individual creates the trust but fails to faithfully place all assets in the trust. This failure effectively neutralizes the probate-avoidance objective of the trust.

Liquidity

For larger estates where estate planning cannot completely avoid the estate tax, provision should be made to pay the taxes without liquidating the estate assets. This is particularly important when the primary asset included in the estate is a family business or farm, making liquidation unacceptable. Adequate life insurance is the most common device for providing this liquidity. Other options that should be considered include the redemption of stock of a family corporation under Sec. 303, and installment payments on the estate tax imposed on certain interests in closely held businesses under Sec. 6166.

COMPUTATION AID: For a worksheet to use when interviewing a client to collect information for estate planning purposes, see Worksheet 5.3 on page 173.

Estate Planning Techniques

Note: The discussion in this section assumes that the date of death is the year 2006 or after. In those years, the applicable credit amount will be $345,800 and the applicable exemption amount will be $1,000,000. If the date of death is sooner, these amounts will be less, as previously outlined.

Couples or Individuals with $1,000,000 or Less

Due to the structure of the unified transfer system, couples with net assets of $1,000,000 or less (smaller applicable unified credit for years earlier than 2006) will pay no federal estate tax. The only transfer tax planning that might be needed would relate to state estate or inheritance taxes.

The primary assistance that the tax advisor can provide is a strong recommendation that the individual execute a will, a durable power of attorney, and an advance directive to physician. A revocable trust might also be considered.

Even with small estates, nontax considerations might warrant estate planning to protect the surviving spouse and other family members. There are some situations where one or both of the spouses might not want his or her assets to pass directly to the surviving spouse. One of the spouses might not be capable of managing the couple's assets. There could be concern that the surviving spouse's remarriage might result in the original couple's assets coming under the control of the new spouse, and consequently not being available for the offspring of the first marriage. In estate planning for a second marriage, one or both of the parties might want to provide for the surviving spouse during his or her lifetime, but want the assets to be available for the offspring of an earlier marriage upon the death of the surviving spouse. In these cases, creation of a trust might be in order.

One option would be the creation of a revocable trust with a provision that all or part of the trust becomes irrevocable upon the death of one of the spouses. Another option would be a testamentary trust created under the will of one or both of the spouses. In either case, the trust could provide for the income of the assets and some limited portion of the assets to be available to the surviving spouse during his or her lifetime, with the remaining assets to be distributed to their beneficiaries upon that spouse's death.

Couples with More than $1,000,000

The most basic estate planning technique is to use both spouses' unified credit by using the marital deduction effectively. This will not be accomplished if all of the assets of the first spouse to die pass freely to the surviving spouse. In this case, the first to die has no net estate due to the marital deduction and no need for the unified credit. However, unless the surviving spouse manages to spend enough of the combined assets to reduce his or her estate to less than $1,000,000, this second spouse's unified credit will not be enough to shield that estate from estate taxes.

One approach would be to leave all of the assets except $1,000,000 (or, if less, enough assets to reduce the second estate to $1,000,000) to the surviving spouse. The marital deduction would reduce the first estate to $1,000,000, and the first unified credit would offset all of the taxes. The second unified credit could then offset up to $1,000,000 of the second estate, with maximum use being made of both unified credits. (A smaller applicable unified credit would apply for years earlier than 2006.)

Except for very large estates, a direct transfer of assets to someone other than the surviving spouse might not be acceptable because the surviving spouse needs the assets, or at least the income from the assets, for living expenses. However, the use of a trust with a terminable interest that does not qualify as qualified terminable interest property could yield the same results. An effective, flexible tool is a qualified terminable interest property trust giving the executor the right to make the election as to how much of the life estate will be treated as qualified terminable interest property qualifying for the marital deduction. The executor will not make the election for the appropriate amount of the property equal to the applicable exemption amount. A proper election will result in just enough property being left in the taxable estate to use up the decedent's applicable unified credit.

If a couple owns all of their property jointly, this technique may not be used successfully. Jointly owned property passes automatically to the surviving owner. This property would qualify for the marital deduction, leaving nothing in the estate of the first spouse to die and everything in the estate of the surviving spouse.

Marital deduction planning cannot be achieved if one of the spouses owns none or very little of the assets of the couple and that spouse dies first. There is no way for that spouse to retain assets to use up his or her unified credit. To facilitate this planning technique, the spouse owning the assets can make appropriate gifts to the other spouse. The unlimited marital deduction will prevent any taxable gifts.

Trusts serve estate planning purposes other than marital deduction planning. A trust with the income to be paid to the surviving spouse and the remaining assets to be paid to the couple's children or other named beneficiaries upon the second death can be used to protect the assets for the benefit of both the surviving spouse and the beneficiaries. Putting the assets in trust keeps the assets out of the control and out of the estate of a subsequent spouse of the decedent's surviving spouse. If the trusts are set up so that they would qualify as qualified terminable interest property if the executor so elects, the executor of the estate can make the proper election to result in a marital deduction that maximizes the use of the couple's applicable unified credits.

EXAMPLES

Mr. and Mrs. Smith have net assets of $1,500,000, owned equally by each spouse. Mrs. Smith dies in 2006, leaving all of her assets directly to Mr. Smith. Mrs. Smith's estate will have no net estate due to the marital deduction. Consequently, Mrs. Smith's unified credit will not be used. If Mr. Smith still has $1,500,000 at death, his estate will owe estate taxes of $210,000 ($555,800 plus 45% of excess over $1,500,000, reduced by Mr. Smith's unified credit of $345,800). (A smaller applicable unified credit will be in effect for years earlier than 2006.)

The same result would be achieved if Mrs. Smith's assets were placed in trust so that the property was treated as qualified terminable interest property and the executor made the election to have the trust so treated. The assets would again qualify for the marital deduction.

Assume instead that Mrs. Smith's assets ($750,000) are placed in trust but that the executor does not make the election to treat the property as qualified terminable interest property. This would leave $750,000 in Mrs. Smith's taxable estate and $750,000 for Mr. Smith. Neither spouse's estate would be large enough to result in an estate tax liability.

As in all cases, the tax advisor should strongly recommend that the individual execute a will, a durable power of attorney and an advance directive to physician. A revocable trust might also be considered.

Individuals with More than $1,000,000

Since there is no marital deduction planning to be done with an unmarried individual, other planning techniques that might be considered include a gifting program, charitable gifts, and generation-skipping transfers.

As in all cases, the tax advisor should strongly recommend that the individual execute a will, a durable power of attorney, and an advance directive to physician. A revocable trust might also be considered.

Couples with More than $2,000,000

In addition to planning to use both spouses' unified credit, other planning techniques that might be considered include a gifting program, charitable gifts, and generation-skipping transfers.

For couples with assets in excess of $2,000,000, another technique would be to leave half of the combined assets with the surviving spouse, taking advantage of the lower marginal tax rates in each estate. This technique would require an evaluation of the deferral benefits of paying higher marginal rates in the second estate but at a later date. Since the benefits of the graduated rates have been eliminated for estates of $10,000,000 or more, this technique would not apply for very large estates.

As in all cases, the tax advisor should strongly recommend that the individual execute a will, a durable power of attorney, and an advance directive to physician. A revocable trust might also be considered.

Grantor Retained Interest Trusts

A *grantor retained interest trust* (GRINT) is a commonly used planning device for relatively large estates and therefore warrants a short discussion. With a GRINT, the grantor establishes an irrevocable trust and retains a property right from the trust for a term of years or until the grantor's death. At the end of that period of time, the trust assets are distributed or remain in trust of the beneficiaries.

A *grantor retained income trust* (GRIT) is an irrevocable trust established with the grantor retaining a use or income interest. A *grantor retained annuity trust* (GRAT) is an irrevocable trust established with the grantor retaining an annuity interest. A *grantor retained unitrust* (GRUT) is an irrevocable trust established with the grantor retaining a percentage of the periodic value of the trust. The remainder interest is a gift to the beneficiaries of the trust.

With GRATs and GRUTs, the amount of the gift is the value of the property placed in trust, less the value of the interest retained by the grantor. (See Sec. 2702.) The longer the term and the greater the value of the retained interest, the smaller the value of the gift and the smaller the amount of the unified credit used or the gift taxes paid. If the grantor survives the trust's fixed term, the trust assets belong to the beneficiary, and all appreciation in value during the trust term is not treated as a gift and is not included in the gross estate of the grantor. On the other hand, if the grantor dies within the trust's fixed term, the full value of the property in the trust is included in the grantor's estate. (See Sec. 2036.) Since these interests are generally valued under Sec. 2702, their use results in transfer tax savings only if the value of the trust assets grows faster than the increases in the interest rates.

EXAMPLE

Mr. Allen transfers $500,000 to a GRAT, retaining the right to receive an annual annuity of $35,000 a year for 10 years. The remainder goes to his children. The value of the remainder interest is determined under Sec. 7520, using 120% of the federal midterm rate. If the factor were based upon an interest rate of 6%, the resulting rate would be 7.2%. Under Reg. Sec. 20.2031-7, Table B, the term-certain remainder factor for 7.2% and 10 years would be 0.498944. The annuity factor would be 6.959 ([1 − .498944]/.072) The value of the retained interest would be $243,569 ($35,000 × 6.959). The amount of the gift would be $256,431 ($500,000 − $243,569). If Mr. Allen survives for more than 10 years, the $500,000 will have been transferred to the children. None of the $500,000 will be included in the estate. If Mr. Allen dies before the trust term expires, the value of the trust on the date of death will be included in his estate.

An interesting type of GRINT is a qualified personal residence trust. Qualified personal residence trusts are exempted from the special valuations rules of Sec. 2702. (See Reg. Sec. 25.2702-5.) Consequently, the retained interest in this type of trust is valued under the more favorable rules of Reg. Sec. 25.2512-5 and Section 7520. An individual's residence is transferred to a trust for a fixed term. At the end of the fixed term, the house becomes the property of the beneficiaries. The individual can continue to live in the residence, with rent being paid after the trust term has expired.

Since the qualified personal residence trust is an exception to Sec. 2702, the lengthy requirements of Reg. Sec. 25.2702-5 should be carefully followed.

EXAMPLE

Mr. Green, who is 65 years old, establishes a qualified personal residence trust for the benefit of his daughter. The property has a current value of $500,000 and the current applicable Sec. 7520 rate is 10%. The trust is established to last until the earlier of 10 years or Mr. Green's death. The actuarial value of Mr. Green's retained interest is $276,345 and the value of his reversionary interest is $81,655. Therefore, the value of the gift Mr. Green makes to his daughter is only $142,000 ($500,000 − $276,345 − $81,655).

If Mr. Green does not survive for 10 years the property will revert back and be included in his estate at its value on that date, less the value of the gift already made—$142,000.

Note: The amounts in this example were computed using factors from Publication 1457. At the date of this printing, that publication is no longer available. The publication is being revised based on the 1990 Census and will be available from the Superintendent of Documents in 1999.

Transferring Ownership of a Closely Held Business

For a discussion of the estate planning aspects of transferring ownership of a closely held business, see Chapter 4 of this book.

Worksheet 5.1   Computation Aid Estate Planning

Gift Tax Formula

Aggregate amount of gifts for the current period   _____

Less: One-half of above amount of gifts to third parties,
if taxpayer and spouse elect gift-splitting   _____

Plus: One-half of gifts made by spouse to third parties,
if gift-splitting is elected   _____

Less: Annual exclusion of $10,000 (or amount adjusted
for inflation for years after 1998) per donee per year for
all gifts of present interests   _____

Less: Charitable contribution deduction   _____

Less: Marital deduction for qualifying gifts to spouse   _____

Equals: Taxable gifts for the period   _____

Plus: Amount of taxable gifts for prior periods   _____

Equals: Total taxable gifts   ==========

Tax on taxable gifts   _____

Less: Tax, at present rates, on total taxable gifts made
in prior periods   _____

Equals: Tax on current period's gifts   _____

Less: Amount of maximum applicable unified credit amount
for this year, reduced by amount of credit previously utilized   _____

Equals: Gift taxes payable for current period   ==========

Worksheet 5.2   Computation Aid Estate Planning

Estate Tax Formula

Gross estate, valued at date of death or alternate valuation date   _____

Less: Debts, administrative and funeral expenses, and losses   _____

Less: Qualified family-owned interest deduction   _____

Less: Charitable contribution deduction   _____

Less: Marital deduction   _____

Equals: Taxable estate   _____

Plus: Adjusted taxable gifts, valued at date-of-gift values   _____

Equals: Tax base   _____

Tentative tax on tax base   _____

Less: Gift taxes paid on post-1976 taxable gifts   _____

Less: Applicable unified credit amount   _____

Less: Credit for state death taxes   _____

Less: Credit for pre-1977 gift tax on transfers included
in gross estate   _____

Less: Credit for tax on prior transfers   _____

Less: Credit for foreign death taxes   _____

Equals: Balance due   _____

Worksheet 5.3   Computation Aid Estate Planning

Planning Worksheet

Assets

Asset Cash Equivalents	Ownership	Amount
Checking accounts		
_____	_____	_____
_____	_____	_____
_____	_____	_____
_____	_____	_____
Savings accounts		
_____	_____	_____
_____	_____	_____
_____	_____	_____
_____	_____	_____
Money market accounts		
_____	_____	_____
_____	_____	_____
_____	_____	_____
_____	_____	_____
Money market fund accounts		
_____	_____	_____
_____	_____	_____
_____	_____	_____
_____	_____	_____
Certificates of deposit		
_____	_____	_____
_____	_____	_____
_____	_____	_____
_____	_____	_____
U.S. Treasury bills		
_____	_____	_____
_____	_____	_____
_____	_____	_____
_____	_____	_____

Worksheet 5.3   Computation Aid Estate Planning (*continued*)

Planning Worksheet

Assets

Assets	Ownership	Amount
Cash value of life insurance		

Investments

Family-owned business interest (corporation, partnership, proprietorship)

Stocks

Bonds

Mutual fund investments

Other investments

(*continues*)

Worksheet 5.3   Computation Aid Estate Planning (*continued*)

Planning Worksheet

Assets

Assets	Ownership	Amount
Real estate		
Principal residence		
Second residence		
Farm/ranch land		
Retirement Fund		
Pension (present lump-sum value)		
IRAs and Keogh accounts		
Employee savings plans (e.g., 401(k), SEP, ESOP)		
Personal Assets		
Automobiles		

Worksheet 5.3   Computation Aid Estate Planning (*continued*)

Planning Worksheet

Assets

Assets	Ownership	Amount
Other assets (furs, jewelry, home furnishings, etc.)		

_____	_____	_____
_____	_____	_____
_____	_____	_____
_____	_____	_____
_____	_____	_____
_____	_____	_____
_____	_____	_____

Total assets   _____

Liabilities

Charge account balances

_____	_____
_____	_____
_____	_____
_____	_____

Personal loans

_____	_____
_____	_____
_____	_____
_____	_____

Student loans

_____	_____
_____	_____

Auto loans

_____	_____
_____	_____

(*continues*)

Worksheet 5.3   Computation Aid Estate Planning (*continued*)

Planning Worksheet

Liabilities

401(k) loans

_____   _____

_____   _____

Investment loans (margin, real estate, etc.)

_____   _____

_____   _____

Home mortgages

_____   _____

_____   _____

Home equity loans

_____   _____

_____   _____

Life insurance policy loans

_____   _____

_____   _____

Projected income tax liability

_____   _____

_____   _____

Other liabilities

_____   _____

_____   _____

_____   _____

_____   _____

Total   _____

Planning Worksheet

Gifts

Date	Donee	Taxable Gift	Gift Tax Paid
Totals			

CHAPTER 5

Marriage and Remarriage

Introduction

A common situation encountered by a tax planner for seniors is the planned marriage of a widow and widower. Some specific issues should be discussed with these individuals *before* the marriage.

The Marriage Penalty

The tax liability of a married couple is generally different than the combined tax liabilities of the two unmarried individuals. The obvious exception is where there is no tax liability as either a married or as two single individuals. One would not expect the relatively small differences in tax liability to affect the couple's decision to marry or not to marry. However, the information might be helpful in the couple's budgeting process and might even affect the timing of the marriage.

In January 1998, the American Institute of Certified Public Accountants (AICPA) issued a phaseout simplification proposal entitled "AICPA Legislative Simplification Proposal on Phase-outs Based on Income Level." The proposal summarized in Table 6.1, identified 20 phaseouts in current law where the total of two single individuals' phaseout amounts do not equal one-half of a married couple's phaseout amounts.

Additional limitations noted by the AICPA where the married limitation does not equal twice the single limitation include:

Sec. 1	Tax rates
Sec. 38	General business credit
Sec. 42	Low-income housing credit
Sec. 62	Certain expenses of qualified performing artist
Sec. 63	Standard deductions
Sec. 86	Social Security benefits
Sec. 125	Cafeteria plans
Sec. 129	Employer child care benefits
Sec. 147	Private activity bonds
Sec. 162	Self-employed health insurance
Sec. 163	Mortgage interest deduction
Sec. 165	Casualty and gambling losses
Sec. 172	Net operating loss
Sec. 179	Election to expense certain business assets
Sec. 194	Reforestation deduction
Sec. 213	Medical expenses
Sec. 220	Medical savings account and limit of high deductible health plan
Sec. 263A	Farm deductions
Sec. 267	Related-party losses
Sec. 318	Constructive ownership of stock

TABLE 6.1 Phaseout Amounts

Sec.	Provision	Married—joint	Single and HOH	Married—separate
21	30% dependent care credit	$10,000–$20,000	$10,000–$20,000	-0-
22	Elderly credit	10,000–25,000	7,500–17,500	5,000–12,500
32	Earned income credit			
	No children	5,570–10,030	10,030	-0-
	One child	12,260–26,473	12,260–26,473	-0-
	Two or more children	12,260–30,095	12,260–30,095	-0-
219	IRA deduction with retirement plan	50,000–60,000	30,000–40,000	-0-
221	Education loan interest expense	60,000–75,000	40,000–55,000	-0-
24	Child credit	110,000*	75,000*	55,000*
25A	Hope and lifetime learning credits	80,000–100,000	40,000–50,000	-0-
23 & 137	Adoption credit/ exclusion	75,000–115,000	75,000–115,000	-0-
55(d)	AMT exemption	150,000–330,000	112,500–247,000	75,000–165,000
68	Itemized deductions	124,000	124,000	62,250
135	EE bond interest exclusion	78,350–108,350	52,250–67,250	-0-
151	Personal and dependency	186,800–309,300	124,500–247,000	93,400–154,650
	HOH		155,650–278,150	
219	IRA spouse nonactive	150,000–160,000	n/a	n/a
408A	Roth IRA	150,000–160,000	95,000–110,000	n/a
408A	IRA to Roth IRA rollover	100,000	100,000	no rollover
469(i)	Rental real estate exception	100,000–150,000	100,000–150,000	50,000–75,000
469(i)	Passive activity credit	200,000–250,000	200,000–250,000	100,000–125,000
530	Education IRA	150,000–160,000	95,000–110,000	n/a

*Upper limit depends on number of children

Sec. 341	Collapsible corporations
Sec. 424	Employee stock options
Sec. 544	Personal ownership in personal holding companies
Sec. 613(C)	Percentage depletion
Sec. 672	Grantor trusts limitations
Sec. 704	Family partnership
Sec. 911	Foreign housing allowance
Sec. 1044	Small-business rollover
Sec. 1092	Straddles
Sec. 1202	Small-business stock rollover
Sec. 1211	Capital loss limitation
Sec. 1223	Short sales
Sec. 1235	Sales of patents
Sec. 1239	Related-party gains
Sec. 1244	Losses in small-business stock
Sec. 1256	Hedging transactions
Sec. 1272	Original issue discount
Sec. 1361	S corporation defined
Sec 1563	Controlled group of corporations
Sec. 6017	Self-employment tax
Sec. 6654	Estimated income tax
Sec. 7872	Below-market loans

COMPUTATION AID: For a worksheet to identify tax provisions that might impact the marriage penalty for specific individuals, see Worksheet 6.1 on page 189.

The marriage penalty usually occurs when the two individuals have somewhat equal incomes. The following simple examples point out the effect of only the standard deduction, tax tables, and the taxation of Social Security benefits.

EXAMPLE

Mr. Smith and Ms. Jones, both age 67, are considering marriage. They each have interest income of $10,000, income from their retirement plans of $20,000, and Social Security benefits of $10,000 annually. As single individuals, they would each have a 1998 tax liability of $4,363, with a combined liability of $8,726, computed as follows:

Interest income	$10,000
Retirement income	20,000
Social Security included in gross income	5,350
Standard deduction	−5,300
Personal exemption	−2,700
Taxable income	$27,350
Tax liability	$ 4,363

Social Security included in gross income:

Lesser of:

- One-half of $10,000 = $5,000

- One-half of ($10,000 + $20,000 + .5[$10,000] − $25,000) = $5,000

Lesser of:

- 85% of $10,000 = $8,500

- Sum of:
    85% of ($10,000 + $20,000 + .5[$10,000] − $34,000) = $850
    Lesser of $5,000 and $4,500 = $4,500
    Sum = $5,350

As a married couple, the tax liability would be $12,079, computed as follows:

(continues)

Interest income	$20,000
Retirement income	40,000
Social Security included in gross income	17,000
Standard deduction	−8,800
Personal exemption	−5,400
Taxable income	$62,800
Tax liability	$12,079

Social Security included in gross income:

Lesser of:

- One-half of $20,000 = $10,000

- One-half of ($20,000 + $40,000 + .5[$20,000] − $32,000) = $16,500

Lesser of:

- 85% of $20,000 = $17,000

- Sum of:
    85% of ($20,000 + $40,000 + .5[$20,000] − $44,000) = $17,850
    Lesser of $10,000 and $6,000 = $6,000
    Sum = $23,850

The difference, $12,079 − $8,726 = $3,353, might make it worth putting off the marriage until early January.

When the incomes of the individuals are unequal, the marriage penalty may become a marriage bonus.

EXAMPLE

Assume that Mr. Smith has no income other than $10,000 of Social Security. Ms. Jones has $10,000 of interest income, $20,000 of income from her retirement plan, and $10,000 of Social Security income. Mr. Smith would have no tax liability, and, as computed above, Ms. Jones would have a tax liability of $4,363, with a combined tax liability of $4,363.

As a married couple, the tax liability would be $2,970, computed as follows:

Interest income	$10,000
Retirement income	20,000
Social Security included in gross income	4,000
Standard deduction	−8,800
Personal exemption	−5,400
Taxable income	$19,800
Tax liability	$ 2,970

Social Security included in gross income:

Lesser of:

- One-half of $20,000 = $10,000

- One-half of ($10,000 + 20,000 + 0.5[$20,000] − $32,000) = $4,000

Consequently, the marriage penalty becomes a marriage bonus with the combined individual liabilities exceeding the married liability by $4,363 − $2,970 = $1,393. In this case, a Christmas marriage might be preferable to a New Year's ceremony.

For a discussion of the taxation of Social Security benefits, see the "Taxation of Social Security Benefits" section in Chapter 3 of this book.

Maximizing Social Security Benefits

If the individuals contemplating marriage are divorcees or widow(er)s, they may be receiving benefits based upon their former spouses' earnings records. For widows and widowers, if the remarriage occurs after age 60, the individual will generally receive the largest of the benefit based on the former spouse's earnings and any benefit to which they are otherwise entitled, including a benefit based upon the new spouse's earnings record. If the benefit currently being received based upon a former spouse's earnings is larger than the other benefits, remarriage might be deferred until after age 60.

Divorced people have great potential for suffering a reduction in benefits because of remarriage. Based on the former spouse's earnings record, a divorced person is entitled to benefits if he or she meets the following conditions:

- Was married to that spouse for at least 10 years

- Is at least 62 years old (60 if the ex-spouse is deceased)

- Is unmarried

- Is not eligible for an equal or higher benefit based on his or her own record, or on someone else's earnings record

If the benefits being received based on an ex-spouse's record are greater than the benefits to be received based on the new spouse's record, the individual will suffer a reduction in benefits.

If the ex-spouse has died, the required age is reduced to 60 years of age (50 if disabled), and remarriage is allowed if the remarriage occurred after age 60 (50 if disabled). In cases of remarriage, the divorcee is eligible for the greater of a widow's benefit on the ex-spouse's record or a spouse's benefit on the new spouse's record. If the benefit based on the ex-spouse's record is greater and the individual is nearing 60 years of age, it might be reasonable to delay the marriage for some period of time.

The most prudent course of action would be for the client to contact the Social Security Administration and have that agency determine the effect of the marriage.

For a discussion of spouse, surviving spouse, and divorced spouse benefits, see the "Social Security Retirement Benefits" section in Chapter 3 of this book.

Estate Planning

The individuals should evaluate their estate plans to take into account their new marital status. The romantic feelings being experienced might preclude the rational financial and estate planning that needs to be done at this time. A rational third party such as their tax advisor can be invaluable in suggesting such things as a prenuptial agreement and other measures to arrange the couple's affairs in a mutually beneficial manner.

Both individuals probably want to ensure that their separate assets and the income therefrom continues to be available for their use. They might even want the income to be available to the surviving spouse upon their eventual death. But in most second marriages, unless they expect offspring from this union, the individuals want their assets to eventually pass to their own heirs and not to the other partner's heirs. A trust, with the income to be paid to the surviving spouse and the remaining assets to be paid to the individual's children or other named beneficiaries upon the second death, can be used to protect the assets for the benefit of the beneficiaries. Estate tax considerations can result in appropriate trusts that maximize the use of the couple's unified credits.

The tax advisor should also recommend that the individuals update their wills, their durable powers of attorney, and their advance directives to physician.

For more discussion of estate planning, see Chapter 5 of this book.

Maximizing the Exclusion on the Gains on the Sale of Both Homes

Both individuals contemplating marriage may own their own home before the marriage. Each individual can exclude up to $250,000 of gain on the sale of a principal residence if they each meet the ownership and use tests for their own homes. Either could elect to exclude up to $500,000 of gain if neither has excluded gain on the sale of a principal residence during the past year. Consequently, the individuals should evaluate the potential gain on each of the houses as early as possible. If one of the houses will yield a gain of more than $250,000 and the other gain will be larger, it might be a good planning strategy to sell the house with the smaller gain now. The couple could live in the other house for the required two years and then exclude up to $500,000 on the sale of the second house.

The tax advisor should determine the values and the individuals' bases in their homes to determine the amount of the potential exclusions. In most of these cases, half of the basis of the home was probably stepped up upon the death of the first spouse. In community property states, the total basis was stepped up to the fair market value.

For further discussion of the exclusion of gain on the sale of a home, see the "Exclusion of Gain on Sale of Principal Residence" section in Chapter 7 of this book.

Worksheet 6.1   Computation Aid Marriage Penalty

Sections Potentially Causing Marriage Penalty to Apply to Client

Section	Provision	Yes
Sec. 21	30 percent dependent care credit	
Sec. 22	Elderly credit	
Sec. 32	Earned income credit	
Sec. 219	IRA deduction with retirement plan	
Sec. 221	Education loan interest expense	
Sec. 24	Child credit	
Sec. 25A	Hope and lifetime learning credits	
Secs. 23 & 137	Adoption credit/exclusion	
Sec. 55(d)	AMT exemption	
Sec. 68	Itemized deductions	
Sec. 135	EE bond interest exclusion	
Sec. 151	Personal and dependency	
Sec. 219	IRA spouse nonactive	
Sec. 408A	Roth IRA	
Sec. 408A	IRA to Roth IRA rollover	
Sec. 469(i)	Rental real estate exception	
Sec. 469(i)	Passive activity credit	
Sec. 530	Education IRA	
Sec. 1	Tax rates	
Sec. 38	General business credit	
Sec. 42	Low-income housing credit	
Sec. 62	Certain expenses of qualified performing artist	
Sec. 63	Standard deductions	
Sec. 86	Social Security benefits	
Sec. 125	Cafeteria plans	

(*continues*)

Worksheet 6.1 Computation Aid Marriage Penalty (*continued*)

Sections Potentially Causing Marriage Penalty to Apply to Client

Section	Provision	Yes
Sec. 129	Employer child care benefits	
Sec. 147	Private activity bonds	
Sec. 162	Self-employed health insurance	
Sec. 163	Mortgage interest deduction	
Sec. 165	Casualty and gambling losses	
Sec. 172	Net operating loss	
Sec. 179	Election to expense certain business assets	
Sec. 194	Reforestation deduction	
Sec. 213	Medical expenses	
Sec. 220	Medical savings account and limit of high deductible health plan	
Sec. 263A	Farm deductions	
Sec. 267	Related party losses	
Sec. 318	Constructive ownership of stock	
Sec. 341	Collapsible corporations	
Sec. 424	Employee stock options	
Sec. 544	Personal ownership in personal holding companies	
Sec. 613(C)	Percentage depletion	
Sec. 672	Grantor trusts limitations	
Sec. 704	Family partnership	
Sec. 911	Foreign housing allowance	
Sec. 1044	Small-business rollover	
Sec. 1092	Straddles	
Sec. 1202	Small-business stock rollover	
Sec. 1211	Capital loss limitation	
Sec. 1223	Short sales	
Sec. 1235	Sales of patents	

Worksheet 6.1   Computation Aid Marriage Penalty (*continued*)

Sections Potentially Causing Marriage Penalty to Apply to Client

Section	Provision	Yes
Sec. 1239	Related party gains	
Sec. 1244	Losses in small business stock	
Sec. 1256	Hedging transactions	
Sec. 1272	Original issue discount	
Sec. 1361	S corporation defined	
Sec. 1563	Controlled group of corporations	
Sec. 6017	Self-employment tax	
Sec. 6654	Estimated income tax	
Sec. 7872	Below-market loans	

Miscellaneous Provisions

Additional Standard Deduction

In general, individuals may choose between itemized deductions or a standard deduction. Individuals are entitled to a higher deduction (basic plus additional standard deductions) if they are age 65 or older on the last day of the year. For this purpose, an individual is considered to be age 65 on the day before his or her sixty-fifth birthday. Consequently, individuals that become 65 on January 1 are considered 65 years of age on the preceding December 31.

The basic and additional standard deduction amounts for 1998 and 1999 are provided in Table 7.1.

In addition to the requirement that the individual be over 65, the additional standard deduction is subject to all of the rules governing the basic standard deduction. Individuals are not eligible for either the basic or the additional deduction if any of the following conditions apply:

TABLE 7.1 Standard Deductions

Basic standard deductions	1998	1999
Single	$4,250	$4,300
Married, filing jointly	7,100	7,200
Surviving spouse	7,100	7,200
Head of household	6,250	6,350
Married, filing separately	3,550	3,600
Additional standard deductions (age 65 or older or blind)	**1998**	**1999**
Single	$1,050	$1,050
Married, filing jointly	850	850
Surviving spouse	850	850
Head of household	1,050	1,050
Married, filing separately	850	850

- The individual is married and filing a separate return and the individual's spouse itemized deductions.

- The individual is filing a short-period tax return due to a change in accounting period.

- The individual is a nonresident alien for all or part of the year.

If the individual can be claimed as a dependent on another person's tax return, the basic standard deduction is limited to the greater of the following amounts:

- $700

- The sum of the individual's earned income and $250, but not to exceed the individual's normal basic standard deduction

The additional standard deduction is added to this amount.

Another additional standard deduction amount may be deducted if the individual is legally blind.

EXAMPLES

Mr. and Ms. Smith, ages 67 and 62, file their tax return as a married couple filing jointly. Their standard deduction for 1999 is $8,050 (the basic standard deduction of $7,200, plus one additional amount of $850).

Ms. Jones, a 70-year-old widow, is claimed as a dependent on her daughter's tax return. She has no earned income. Ms. Jones's standard deduction for 1999 is $1,750 (the basic standard deduction of $700, plus one additional amount of $1,050).

As a result of these standard deduction amounts and the 1998 exemption amount of $2,700, taxpayers are required to file a tax return in 1998 if their gross income exceeds the amounts listed in Table 7.2.

As a result of these standard deduction amounts and the 1999 exemption amount of $2,750, taxpayers are required to file a tax return in 1999 if their gross income exceeds the amounts listed in Table 7.3.

These amounts are the sum of the individuals' basic standard deduction, additional standard deduction, and personal exemption. Consequently, for individuals who may be claimed as a dependent on another individual's tax return, these amounts must be reduced to reflect the $700 basic standard deduction as previously explained.

TABLE 7.2 Gross Income Filing Threshold—1998

Filing status	Gross income
Single—over 65	$8,000
Head of household—over 65	$10,000
Married filing jointly	
One spouse over 65	$13,350
Both spouses over 65	$14,200
Married filing separately	$2,700

TABLE 7.3 Gross Income Filing Threshold—1999

Filing status	Gross income
Single—over 65	$8,100
Head of household—over 65	$10,150
Married filing jointly	
One spouse over 65	$13,550
Both spouses over 65	$14,400
Married filing separately	$2,750

In addition, the following individuals must file a tax return:

- Employers of a domestic employer paying more than $1,100 per year and required to file Schedule H—Household Employment Taxes

- Individuals with self-employment income of more than $400

- Individuals with income of $108.28 or more from a church or qualified church-controlled organization that is exempt from employer Social Security and Medicare taxes

- Individuals who owe Social Security and Medicare taxes on unreported tips

- Individuals who owe Social Security and Medicare taxes on group term life insurance

- Individuals who owe alternative minimum tax

- Individuals who owe excise or penalty taxes on a qualified retirement plan or an individual retirement plan

- Individuals who owe taxes from the recapture of the investment tax credit or various other credits

Credit for the Elderly and Disabled

The tax credit for the elderly and the disabled is available to an individual who is 65 years of age. It is also available to an individual who is under age 65, who retired without having reached mandatory retirement age, and who was permanently and totally disabled at retirement. (See Sec. 22(b).)

The credit is structured to benefit individuals who receive moderate amounts of Social Security; railroad retirement; and other pension, annuity, or disability benefits and who have modest amounts of income from other sources. This is accomplished using the following formula:

Initial amount

Less:	Nontaxable retirement benefits
Less:	One-half of excess of adjusted gross income over certain amounts
Equals:	Amount subject to credit
Multiply by:	15%
Equals:	Amount of credit

In determining the credit, individuals age 65 or older begin with an initial amount, depending upon filing status. The initial amounts are:

Single	$5,000
Married filing jointly	$7,500
Married filing separately	$3,500

The initial amount is reduced dollar for dollar by any amounts received as nontaxable Social Security benefits and nontaxable railroad retirement benefits treated as Social Security, by nontaxable veterans' benefits, and by any other pension, annuity, or disability benefit that is excluded from income.

The initial amount must also be reduced on a dollar-for-dollar basis for one-half of the amount by which an individual's adjusted gross income for the year exceeds the following amounts:

Single	$7,500
Married filing jointly	10,000
Married filing separately	5,000

Consequently, no credit is available if the taxpayer has an adjusted gross income of the following amounts or more or receives the following amounts or more in nontaxable Social Security, railroad retirement, or veterans' benefits or pension, annuity, or disability benefits that are excluded from gross income:

	AGI exceeds	Nontaxable benefits
Single	$17,500	$5,000
Married filing jointly— both eligible	25,000	7,500
Married filing jointly— one spouse eligible	20,000	5,000
Married filing separately	12,500	3,750

EXAMPLES

Ms. Allen, age 66 and single, has an adjusted gross income (AGI) of $8,500 and receives $4,000 of nontaxable Social Security benefits for the year. Her credit would be computed as follows:

Initial amount	$5,000
Less: Social Security benefits	4,000
Reduced initial amount	$1,000
Less: One-half of AGI above $7,500	500
Amount eligible for credit	$ 500
Credit: $500 × 15%	$ 75

Mr. and Mrs. Brown, both age 66, file a joint return, have an adjusted gross income of $10,000, and receive combined nontaxable Social Security benefits of $6,000. Their credit would be computed as follows:

Initial amount	$7,500
Less: Social Security benefits	6,000
Reduced initial amount	$1,500
Less: One-half of AGI above $10,000	-0-
Amount eligible for credit	$1,500
Credit: $1,500 × 15%	$ 225

Exclusion of Gain on Sale of Principal Residence

Introduction

The Taxpayer Relief Act of 1997 repealed the one-time election to exclude gain of up to $125,000 on the sale of an individual's principal residence and the rollover of gain into the basis of a replacement residence if such replacement residence is acquired within two years of the sale. (See P. L. 105-34; former Secs. 121 and 1034.) For sales of a residence after May 6, 1997, gains of up to $250,000 ($500,000 for married individuals filing jointly) may be excluded. (See Sec. 121.)

The individual excluding a gain must meet ownership and use requirements.

Ownership and Use Tests

During the five-year period ending on the date of the sale, the individual must have owned the residence for at least two years, and the individual must have lived in the residence for at least two years. (See Sec. 121 (a)(2).) The tests do not have to be met at the same time, but both must be met during the five-year period. Neither test requires that the time period be continuous. The tests are met if the individual owned and lived in the house for 24 full months or 730 days during the five-year period. Short temporary absences for vacations or other seasonal absences, even if you rent out the property during the absences, are counted as periods of use. (See Reg. Sec. 1.121-1(c).)

If the acquisition of the home being sold resulted in the non-recognition of gain under Sec. 1034 (the old rollover provision), the ownership and use periods include the ownership and use of the prior residence. The use and ownership of each previously owned residence (taken into account under Sec. 1223(7)) whose gains were ultimately rolled over into the residence are also included. (See Sec. 121(g).)

If the basis of the home being sold was determined under Sec. 1033 due to the fact that the home was acquired to replace another home disposed of in an involuntary conversion, special rules apply for the use and ownership tests. To determine whether the individual meets the use and ownership tests, the time the individual owned and lived in the involuntarily converted residence is added to the time the individual owned and lived in the replacement residence. (See Sec. 121(d)(5)(C).)

There is an exception to the ownership and use tests if an individual becomes physically or mentally incapable of self-care at any time during the five-year period ending on the date of the sale or exchange of a principal residence. If that person resides in a nursing home or similar facility while still owning the home and met the ownership and use tests for at least one year, the two-year use and ownership tests will be satisfied. (See Sec. 121(d)(6).)

A reduced exclusion is available for individuals who fail to meet the two-year use and ownership tests because the sale or exchange is by reason of one of the following circumstances:

- A change in place of employment
- A change in health

- Unforeseen circumstances, to the extent to be provided in regulations

The $250,000 or $500,000 exclusion is reduced to the amount not exceeding the amount that bears the same ratio to the full exclusion as the shorter of either of the following periods bears to two years:

- The aggregate periods, during the five-year period ending on the date of the sale or exchange, that the property has been owned and used as the principal residence.

- The period between the most recent sale or exchange resulting in an exclusion under this provision and the current sale or exchange

(See Sec. 121(c).)

EXAMPLES

From Year 1 through Year 4, Mr. Smith lived with his son and daughter-in-law in a house owned by his son. On January 5, Year 4, he bought this house from his son. He continued to live there until May 5, Year 5, when he sold it. Although Mr. Smith lived in the property as his principal residence for more than two years, he cannot claim a full exclusion for his gain on the sale. He did not own the property for the required two years. However, if the reason for the sale was a change in employment, health, or an acceptable unforeseen circumstance, he could exclude up to $166,667 ($^{16}/_{24} \times$ $250,000) of gain on the sale. He lived in the house for 16 months.

Professor Mary Jones bought and moved into a house on January 4, Year 1. She lived in it as her principal residence continuously until February 4, Year 2, when she went abroad for a one-year sabbatical leave. During part of the period of leave, the property was unoccupied, and during the rest of the period she rented it out. On March 4, Year 3, she sold the house and purchased another house in the same general

(continues)

area. Because her leave was not a short temporary absence, she cannot include the period of leave to meet the test of living in the house as her principal residence for two or more years. She cannot exclude her gain from the sale of the house. However, if she accepted a new teaching position in another city and purchased a new home, she would be able to exclude a portion of the gain. She owned the old home for over two years, but she only lived in it for 11 months, so she could exclude only a portion of the $250,000 exclusion. The exclusion ratio is $^{11}/_{24}$, the ratio of the time she met the ownership and use requirements to the required two-year (24-month) period.

In Year 1, Mr. Wilson was 50 years old and lived in a rented apartment. The apartment building was later changed to a condominium, and he bought his condominium unit on December 1, Year 4. In Year 5, Mr. Wilson became ill, and on April 14, Year 5, he moved to his daughter's home. On February 14, Year 7, while still living in his daughter's home, he sold his condominium unit. Mr. Wilson can claim an exclusion of up to $250,000 of the gain on the sale of his condominium unit. The five-year test period is from February 15, Year 2 to February 14, Year 7. He owned his condominium unit from December 1, Year 4 to February 14, Year 7, a period of over two years. He lived in the condominium unit from February 15, Year 2 to April 14, Year 5, a period of over two years.

Joint Ownership of Home by a Married Couple

A gain on the sale of a home of up to $500,000 may be excluded by a married couple filing jointly if:

- Either spouse meets the ownership test

- Both spouses meet the use test, and neither spouse is ineligible for exclusion because of a sale or exchange of a residence within the last two years. (See Sec. 121(b)(2).)

When married individuals file a joint tax return, they will be eligible for the $250,000 exclusion if either spouse meets the ownership and use requirements. They would be eligible for a prorated portion of the exclusion if either spouse is entitled to the aforementioned proration. Each spouse may exclude up to $250,000 of gain from the sale of that spouse's principal residence on a joint return if each spouse would be permitted to exclude up to $250,000 of gain if they filed separate returns. (See Committee reports for Act Sec. 312, P.L. 105-34.)

For purposes of the ownership and use tests, a surviving spouse may include the period that the deceased spouse owned and used the property if both of the following conditions apply:

- The deceased spouse died on or before the date of the sale of the principal residence.

- The surviving spouse has not remarried. (See Sec. 121(d)(2).)

Other Effects of Marital Status

If a residence is transferred to an individual from a spouse as a gift, or from a former spouse incident to a divorce, no gain or loss is recognized. (See Sec. 1041(a).) After such a transfer, the spouse or former spouse to whom the residence is transferred can include the period the transferor owned the property for purposes of the ownership test. (See Sec. 121.)

In a divorce, one spouse is sometimes granted use of the couple's home while the other spouse retains ownership of the home. If the spouse retaining ownership of the home eventually sells the home, the spouse with ownership will be treated as having used the home as a principal residence for the period of time the other spouse is granted the right to use the house. (See Sec. 121(d)(3).)

Taxability of Gain to Extent of Depreciation

The exclusion does not apply to the extent of depreciation allowable with respect to the rental or business use of the principal use. This provision applies only to depreciation adjustments after May 6, 1997. (See Sec. 121(d)(6).) This portion of the gain included in gross income will generally be taxed at a maximum rate of 25%. (See Sec. 1.)

Joint Ownership of Home by Other Than a Married Couple

If joint owners of a home are other than husband and wife, each owner who chooses to exclude gain from income must meet the ownership and use tests. If one owner meets the tests, that does not automatically qualify the other owner(s) to exclude their gain from income. Each owner excludes gain on an individual basis. A choice by one owner does not affect the treatment of gain by the other owner(s), either on this home on or the future sale of other homes. (See Rev. Rul. 67-235 1967-2 CB 79.)

Multiple Exclusions Allowed

Unlike the predecessor to Sec. 121, there is no limit on the number of times the exclusion may be claimed. However, the exclusion can be claimed only if, during the two-year period preceding the date of the sale or exchange, there was no other sale or exchange to which this exclusion applied. This provision will be applied without regard to any sale or exchange before May 7, 1997.

EXAMPLES

Mr. and Ms. Smith are married. Mr. Smith sells his separately owned residence and makes an election under Sec. 121(a) to exclude the gain on the sale. Subsequently, Mr. and Ms. Smith divorce. Mr. Smith marries Ms. Jones. Shortly thereafter, Ms. Jones-Smith sells her residence. Because Ms. Jones-Smith has not taken the exclusion during the last two years, she can now exclude the gain if she meets the ownership and use requirements. However, if Mr. Smith sells his new residence, he can exclude the gain only if two years have passed since the last sale.

Mr. Johnson and Ms. Wilson were single and each owned a home. Each met the ownership and use tests. On August 1, Year 1, Ms. Wilson sold her home and excluded a gain of $225,000. In October of Year 1, Mr. Johnson and Ms. Wilson married. If Mr. Johnson sells his home before August 1 of Year 3, he can exclude only $250,000 of gain. This

---

is true whether they file a joint return or separate returns. However, if they wait until the two-year period has passed since Ms. Wilson-Johnson sold her home, the couple can file a joint return and exclude up to $500,000 of gain.

Involuntary Conversions upon Reinvestment in a New Home

Involuntary conversions are treated as sales of property for purposes of this exclusion. Consequently, when gain is excluded under Sec. 121, the amount required to be reinvested to avoid gain recognition under the involuntary conversion provisions is reduced by the amount of gain excluded under Sec. 121. If the basis of the new residence is determined (in whole or in part) under the involuntary conversion provisions, then the holding and use of the converted property is treated as holding and use of the replacement property when it is later sold or exchanged. (See Sec. 121(d)(5).)

EXAMPLE

Mr. Smith's residence burns to the ground, and he receives insurance proceeds of $410,000. He has a basis of $65,000 for the residence. His total gain is $345,000. He is single and meets the use and ownership requirements of Sec. 121. He builds a smaller home, using only $300,000.

If Mr. Smith meets the use and ownership requirements, he will exclude $250,000 of the gain under Sec. 121. The amount realized, the amount required to be reinvested under Sec. 1033, is $160,000 ($410,000 − $250,000.) Since Mr. Smith has reinvested more than $160,000, the remaining gain of $95,000 ($345,000 − $250,000) will be deferred and the basis in his new residence will be reduced by the same amount. His basis in his new home will be $205,000 ($300,000 − $95,000).

Tenant-Stockholder in Cooperative Housing Corporation

The use tests will be applied to the house or apartment that an individual is entitled to occupy as a shareholder of a cooperative housing corporation. The ownership test will be applied to the ownership of the stock. (See Sec. 121(d)(4).)

Sale of Remainder Interests

Although this provision may be applied to the sale of a remainder interest in a principal residence, there is a significant exception. The sale of the remainder interest cannot be made to any person who bears a relationship to the individual described in Secs. 267(b) or 707(b). The relationships include related corporations, partnerships, and trusts, and brothers, sisters, spouses, ancestors, and lineal descendants. (See Sec. 121(d)(8).)

Election to Have Section Not Apply

The individual may elect to not have this section apply. (See Sec. 121(e).)

Sales within Two Years of Enactment

In certain cases, the partial exclusion previously discussed may be claimed even though the use and ownership tests are not satisfied and the sale was not due to a change in employment, health, or an acceptable unforeseen circumstance. The exclusion may be taken if the following conditions apply:

- The individual held the property on August 5, 1997
- The sale or exchange occurs before August 5, 1999. (See Act Sec. 312(d)(3), P. L. 105-34.)

Medical Expenses

General Deductible Medical Expenses

Seniors are subject to the same rules as other taxpayers for deductible medical expenses. Deductible medical expenses include:

- Fees for medical services

- Fees for hospital services

- Insurance premiums paid for medical and dental care or for long-term care

- Meals and lodging provided by a hospital during medical treatment

- Special equipment, such as a motorized wheelchair

- Special items such as false teeth, eyeglasses, hearing aids, crutches, and artificial limbs

- Transportation and lodging for needed medical care

- Prescribed medicines and drugs, and insulin

The sum of medical and dental expenses must be reduced by 7.5% of adjusted gross income.

There are some expenses commonly incurred by seniors that may not be common to other taxpayers. The following paragraphs include specific discussions of medical expenses that might relate specifically to seniors.

Medical Insurance Premiums

Generally, medical insurance premiums are deductible if the policies cover medical care. These policies include those that pay for:

- Hospitalization, surgery, X-rays, and similar fees

- Prescription drugs

- Contact lenses replacement

- Services of doctors, dentists, and other medical practitioners

Medicare A premiums are not deductible medical expenses if the individual is receiving Social Security benefits or is a government employee who paid Medicare tax. Individuals who are not receiving Social Security benefits or are not a government employee who paid Medicare tax, but have voluntarily enrolled in Medicare A, may deduct the premiums as a medical expense.

Medicare B premiums are deductible medical expenses.

Medical and Dental Expenses

Deductible medical expenses generally include payments for medical services provided by physicians, surgeons, specialists, and other medical practitioners. In addition, payments for hospital services, therapy and nursing services, ambulances, and laboratory, surgical, obstetrical, diagnostic, dental, and X-ray fees are deductible.

The portion of fees paid to a retirement home for medical care is deductible. All of the cost of a nursing home is deductible if the main reason for being there is to get medical care.

Wages and other amounts spent for nursing services are deductible. These services include services connected with caring for the patient's condition, such as giving medication, changing dressings, bathing and grooming, and any other service generally performed by a nurse. The person giving the care does not have to be a nurse. Amounts spent for personal and household care unrelated to the patient's condition are not deductible medical expenses.

Special Items and Equipment

Deductible items in this category include payments for:

- False teeth, artificial limbs, eyeglasses, contact lenses, hearing aids and the batteries to operate them, and crutches

- Special equipment for the hearing-impaired or visually impaired and individuals with other incapacities, including:

  Guide dogs or other animals

  Special telephone equipment

  Specially equipped televisions and the cost of the adapter to provide subtitles

Marginal costs of braille books and magazines

Oxygen and oxygen equipment

Special hand controls and other special equipment installed in a car

Wheelchairs for the relief of a sickness or disability

Transportation Costs

Costs paid for transportation primarily for, and essential to, medical care are deductible medical expenses. In addition to expenses necessary to transport the individual to locations where medical services are provided, transportation expenses of a nurse or other provider giving injections, medication, and other treatments would be included as medical expenses. These expenses would include:

- Actual automobile expenses or an optional mileage rate of 10 cents a mile. Actual expenses for this purpose do not include depreciation, insurance or repairs and maintenance.

- Bus, tax, train, or air fares.

Meals and Lodging

Meals and lodging provided by a hospital or similar institution are medical expenses if the individual's primary reason for being in the hospital is to receive medical care. The cost of lodging other than that provided by a hospital and while away from home for necessary medical expenses are deductible if the following conditions apply:

- The lodging is primarily for, and essential to, medical care.

- The medical care is provided by a doctor, a hospital, or a medical care facility related to a hospital.

- The lodging is not lavish or extravagant.

- There is no significant element of personal pleasure, recreation, or vacation in the travel away from home.

The deduction is limited to $50 per night for the person receiving the medical care and $50 per night for a person traveling with the person receiving the medical care.

Capital Expenditures

To the extent that they do not increase the value of your home, special equipment or other improvements to your home to relieve a medical condition are deductible medical expenses. Examples include:

- Central air-conditioning to relieve allergies

- An elevator for an individual suffering from heart disease

- Ramps, widened doorways and hallways, and relocated cabinets, electrical outlets, and so forth for an individual in a wheelchair

- Railings, support bars, handrails, or grab bars.

Multiple-Support Agreements, Head of Household Status, and Medical Expense Deduction of Children Supporting a Parent

Multiple-Support Agreements

The children of an elderly parent may find it necessary to share the cost of providing all or a portion of the parent's support. Although no one individual contributes more than half of the parent's support, one individual may still claim a dependency exemption as one of a group of individuals who have collectively contributed more than half of the support. (See Code Sec. 152(c).) The following conditions must be met:

- Each member of the group would have been entitled to claim the individual as a dependent but for the fact that the support test was not met.

- The member of the group claiming the dependency exemption has contributed more than 10% of the support.

- Each member of the group who contributed more than 10% of support (except the individual claiming the exemption) files a written declaration on Form 2120 that he or she will not claim the individual as a dependent for that tax year.

If more than one-half of a dependent's support is furnished by one individual, that individual is the only one who can claim the dependency deduction. Otherwise, the members of the group may take turns claiming the deduction.

Head of Household Status

Generally, a head of household is an unmarried person who paid more than half the cost of maintaining a home that is his or her principal home and the principal residence for a qualifying individual. The household must constitute the principal residence for that qualifying individual for more than one-half of the tax year. If a taxpayer maintains a home for a dependent parent, the home must be the parent's principal residence for the entire year. For this purpose, a home or household for the parents may include a rest home or home for the aged. This requirement is met if a child pays more than half of the cost of maintaining a parent in a rest home or a home for the aged. (See *J. Robinson,* 51 TC 520, 1968.)

It should be noted that, for purposes of using the head-of-household rate, one child must actually bear more than half the cost of maintaining the household. (See Reg. Sec. 1.2-2(b)(4).) If the cost is divided evenly among the group, no one will be able to claim the status of head of household. The best tax advantage can be gained if a single child with the greatest income qualifies as the head of the household.

Medical Expenses

An individual may deduct another person's medical expenses only if that person meets three of the tests for claiming the dependency exemption. The tests that must be met are the *citizenship, relationship,* and *support* tests. (See Sec. 213(a).) The individual entitled to claim a parent as a dependent under a multiple-support agreement should pay the parent's medical expenses, since the other parties to the multiple-support agreement may not deduct any medical expenses paid for the parent. In addition to being deductible as medical expenses, payment of these expenses is considered part of the dependent's support for purposes of the dependency exemption.

Death Benefit

The death benefit $5,000 exclusion was repealed by the Small Business Protection Act of 1996. (See P.L. 104-188.) The repeal applies to decedents dying after August 20, 1996.

A death benefit received after August 20, 1996, might be successfully excluded as a gift. In the estate of Sydney J. Carter, the following criteria were necessary to excluded a death benefit as a gift:

- The payment was made to the employee's family rather than to the employee's estate.

- The employer received no benefit from the payment.

- The employee's family did not perform services for the employer.

- The decedent had been fully compensated for services rendered so that there was no possibility that the payment was for services.

- The payment was made pursuant to a board of directors' resolution that followed a general company policy of providing payments for families of deceased employees. (See 29 AFTR2d 332, 453 F.2d 61(CA-2, 1972).)

Exclusions

Disability Income

Amounts received as disability payments are included in income to the extent they are due to premiums paid by an individual's employer. Amounts received as disability payments are excluded from income to the extent they are due to premiums paid by the individual. (See Sec. 105(a).)

Railroad Retirement

Benefits paid under the Railroad Retirement Act fall into two categories. These categories are treated differently for income tax purposes.

Tier 1 Benefits

Tier 1 retirement benefits are the amount of the annuity under the Railroad Retirement Act of 1974 equal to the amount of the benefit to which the taxpayer would have been entitled under the Social Security Act if all of the service after December 31, 1936, of the employee had been included as employment under the Social Security Act. This amount is treated as a Social Security benefit and is potentially taxable as such. (See Sec. 86.) Also see the "Taxation of Social Security Benefits" section in Chapter 1 of this book.

Tier 2 Benefits

Tier 2 retirement benefits are treated as amounts received from a qualified retirement plan. The sum of employee contributions to the tier 2 benefits and the nontaxable portion of tier 1 benefits may be recovered tax-free under the rules applicable to qualified plans and annuities. (See Sec. 72(r).) Also see the "Taxation of Periodic Payments—Annuities" section in Chapter 2 of this book.

Military Retirement

If any of the following conditions are met, the amount of a military pension based on percentage of disability will not be included in gross income:

- Before September 25, 1975, the individual was entitled to receive a disability payment.

- On September 24, 1975, the individual was a member of a government service or its reserve component, or was under a binding, written commitment to become a member.

- The individual receives a disability payment because of a combat-related injury.

- If an application were filed, the individual would be entitled to receive disability compensation from the Veterans Administration. (See Sec. 104.)

Life Insurance and Endowment Contract Proceeds

Life Insurance

The proceeds from a life insurance policy that are paid by reason of the death of the insured are generally excluded from gross income. This exclusion is not available if the policy has been transferred for valuable consideration. (See Code Sec. 101.)

If the insurance proceeds are paid in installments, a portion of each payment must be treated as interest. The deemed interest portion of the payments is included in income. The interest portion of the installment payments is any amount above the value of the policy as of the time of the decedent's death. This deemed interest is apportioned among the installment payments. (See Reg. Sec. 1.101-4.)

EXAMPLE

Upon Mrs. Johnson's death, Mr. Johnson has an option of receiving $100,000, the face value of Mrs. Johnson's life insurance policy, in a lump sum or of receiving 10 annual installments of $12,000 each. Mr. Johnson elects to accept the installment payments. Of each $12,000 payment, one-tenth of the $100,000 face value ($10,000 per year) is excludable from his gross income. He is required to include $2,000 of each annual installment payment in his gross income.

In addition to the exclusion of life insurance proceeds upon the death of the insured, life insurance, primarily some form of whole life insurance, offers other tax benefits:

- When amounts are distributed before the insured's death, the distributions are generally first treated as a return of capital and nontaxable, with any excess treated as gain.

- Earnings under the policy are tax-deferred.

- Loans against the policy are generally not considered to be distributions. (See Sec. 72(e).)

Endowment Contracts

Endowment policies mature after a certain number of years or when the insured reaches a certain age. At that time, the policyholder is entitled to the face amount of the policy. The individual often has the choice to receive the total face amount in one payment or to receive an annuity.

Provisions contained in the 1984 Tax Act severely limit the use of endowment policies as an investment. For any modified endowment contract entered into or substantially modified after June 20, 1988, the following provisions apply:

- Loans under the contract are considered to be distributions.

- Distributions before the policy's maturity are first considered earnings, with any excess being treated as nontaxable return of capital. (See Sec. 72(e).)

An endowment contract is a *modified endowment contract* if it meets the definition in Sec. 7702A. Generally, the cumulative amount of premiums paid during the first seven years must not exceed the amount that net level premiums would have been if the policy had provided for paid-up benefits after the payment of seven such level payments. (See Sec. 7702A.)

Tax Consequences of Volunteerism

The value of services provided is not a deductible charitable contribution. Only the out-of-pocket expenses incurred in providing services for a qualified charitable organization are deductible. (See Reg. Sec. 1.170A-1.)

Automobile Expenses

Unreimbursed expenses directly related to the use of an individual's automobile while performing services for a charitable organization are deductible. Only the direct expenses of operating the vehicle are deductible. These direct expenses include the cost of oil and gas. A standard mileage rate of 14 cents a mile may be used in lieu of the actual expenses. (See Sec. 170(2).)

In addition to the direct expenses, whether actual or standard mileage, parking fees and tolls may also be deducted. The miles included in computing the deduction include the distance from the individual's home to the place where the service is done. (See Rev. Rul. 56-508 1956-2 CB 126.)

Travel Expenses

Travel expenses incurred while an individual is away from home performing services for a charitable organization are deductible. The travel must not involve a significant element of personal pleasure, recreation, or vacation. (See Reg. Sec. 1.170A-1.)

Attendance versus Service

Merely attending church or attending a convention will not result in the deductibility of the expenses. The individual must be performing a service for the organization. A chosen representative to a convention is performing such a service. (See Rev. Rul. 61-46 1961-1 CB 51.)

The Social Security Domestic Employment Reform Act of 1994–"The Nanny Tax"

Introduction

Prior to October 22, 1994, Sec. 3401 and related regulations required that employers of household employees with wages of more than $50 per quarter withhold Social Security and Medicare taxes and file quarterly returns on Form 942. Due to the difficulties encountered by several Clinton appointees in the confirmation process because of unpaid Social Security and Medicare taxes, Congress in 1992 began the process of reforming this outdated, harsh, probably unfair, and almost certainly one of the most widely violated provisions of the Internal Revenue Code. This process was consummated October 22, 1994, when President Clinton signed into law The Social Security Domestic Employment Reform Act of 1994 (SSDERA), better known as the "Nanny Tax Reform Act."

New Requirements

SSDERA makes several changes in the treatment of the Social Security and Medicare provisions for domestic help. The most important are as follows:

- The $50 per quarter requirement is replaced with a $1,000 annual threshold, indexed annually after 1997. Any employee making less than this amount will no longer be subject to Social Security and Medicare taxes. This change became effective for 1994.

- Employers of household employees are no longer required to file Form 942 for those employees who are paid more than $1,000 ($1,100 for 1998) per year, nor will they file Form 940 for federal unemployment taxes (FUTA). Social Security, Medicare, and FUTA taxes due are reported on Schedule H, Form 1040 and paid with the employer's Form 1040 effective for 1995 and thereafter.

- Effective for years 1995 and thereafter, employees under the age of 18 will be exempt from Social Security and Medicare taxes unless household employment is the employee's principal business.

Full-time students would be exempt, since being a student would be considered their principal occupation. However a person 17 years of age who had left school to work as a full-time domestic would be subject to withholding and reporting. (See Sec. 3121(b).)

Estimated Tax Requirements

Starting in 1998 employers will be required to include Social Security, Medicare, and FUTA taxes for domestic workers (both employee and employer shares) in calculating their estimated tax for the year. (See Sec. 3510(b)(4).)

Other Provisions

It should be noted that while SSDERA simplifies the reporting for FUTA taxes for domestic employees, it does not change the thresholds for these taxes. FUTA taxes are due if the employer paid household wages of $1,000 or more during any calendar quarter of the current or preceding year. Taxable wages are limited to $7,000 per employee. SSDERA does not change the reporting for state unemployment statutes where quarterly reports may still be required.

Conclusion

The new requirements of SSDERA should make reporting much simpler for most employers. More important, the higher, more realistic threshold and simplified reporting requirements should improve compliance with this often ignored provision of the tax law.

Change of Domicile to Avoid State Income and Estate Taxes

Since the state taxation of income and of estates differ, it is possible that upon retirement individuals may want to move to a state with low tax rates. The laws of both the original state of domicile and the new state should be evaluated. For example, if the individual has a retirement plan, both the state where the retirement fund was accumulated and the state where the income will be received should be reviewed to determine the eventual taxation of the distributions from the retirement plan.

Ownership of property in several states could result in required probate in each of those states. Transfer of the property to a corporation owned by the individual could avoid this multiple probate. Again, the probate laws of the various states should be examined.

Index